SAVING WOTTON

THE REMARKABLE STORY OF
A SOANE COUNTRY HOUSE

Curated by William Palin

SIR JOHN SOANE'S MUSEUM

Saving Wotton: the remarkable story of a Soane country house
an exhibition at Sir John Soane's Museum
2 July – 25 September 2004

Published in Great Britain 2004
by Sir John Soane's Museum
Reg. Charity No.313609
www.soane.org

ISBN 0 9542284 7 2

Supported by
The J Paul Getty Charitable Trust

**COUNTRY LIFE
PICTURE LIBRARY**

The Trustees of Sir John Soane's Museum would like to thank the benefactors, patrons and sponsors whose annual donations support the Museum's exhibition and education programmes.

CORPORATE BENEFACTORS
Bradford and Bingley

PATRONS
Arnold Burton Alan and Ciannait Tait April and Roddy Gow Laurence and Janet Kinney
Clare and Richard Gapper William Parker Lisbet Rausing Richard and Sheila Griffiths
John W Murray Alex and Elinor Sainsbury Nicholas and Elodie Stanley Michael Wilson
Robin and Ann Purchas Jane Wilson Crispin Kelly Leopold de Rothschild
David and Molly Borthwick Peter Hall Rick Mather Mallet Sir Richard MacCormac
Debby and James Brice John and Rowena Jackson The Lady Foley Richard and Rosemary Miller

RECENT EXHIBITION SPONSORS
The Designation Challenge Fund *'Hooked on Books: The Library of Sir John Soane, Architect 1753–1837'*
The Heritage Lottery Fund *'William West and the Regency Toy Theatre'*
The Baring Foundation *'Architecture Unshackled': George Dance the Younger 1741–1825*
Howard de Walden Estates Limited *'Bob the Roman': Heroic Antiquity and the Architecture of Robert Adam*
Henry Moore Foundation *John Flaxman: Master of the Purest Line*

*For information on exhibition sponsorship and how to support the Museum as an individual Patron
or through a company, trust or foundation please contact the development office at
Sir John Soane's Museum, 13 Lincoln's Inn Fields, London WC2A 3BP, England. Tel: 020 7440 4241*

Designed and typeset in Albertina by Libanus Press, Marlborough
Printed by BAS Printers Limited, Salisbury

CONTENTS

Wotton House, the entrance front © Paul Barker/ *Country Life* Picture Library, 2004

PREFACE

Wotton is a great survivor – history has dealt it a number of blows and each time the house has recovered and blossomed. In 1820, when fire struck, John Soane was employed to direct its resurrection, something he achieved with customary skill and originality. A hundred years later the house suffered the indignity of being abandoned altogether, and the heroic intervention by Elaine Brunner at this critical time forms the second part of Wotton's great survival story.

This tercentenary exhibition recounts Wotton's changing fortunes and examines in detail what was one of Soane's most important country house commissions. With Soane's drawings forming the core of the material in this exhibition, it is fitting that it should be held in his Museum. I would like to thank the contributors to this catalogue: David Gladstone; Kate Graham; Donald Insall; Peter Inskip; Michael Portillo and Dr Giles Worsley, and *Country Life* and *Apollo* for allowing us to include versions of published articles. I have been greatly assisted in this project by Susan Palmer, the Soane Museum Archivist; Isabelle Flour, my assistant; Margaret Schuelein who has conserved and mounted the material for display, and Ptolemy Dean whose advice and support have been invaluable. I would also like to thank the lenders, Buckinghamshire County Museum and the Wormsley Library; and the J Paul Getty Charitable Trust and *Country Life* Picture Library for supporting the exhibition.

Lastly, this exhibition could not have happened without the generosity and enthusiasm of April and David Gladstone, the present owners and occupiers of Wotton. We thank them and wish them well with the continuing restoration of the house and grounds.

WILLIAM PALIN
Assistant Curator
Sir John Soane's Museum

The Hall as altered by A S G Butler in 1926 © *Country Life* Picture Library

FOREWORD

THE RT HON. MICHAEL PORTILLO MP

I first came across Wotton some years ago as a tourist. It was open to the public only at limited times, probably because, as I soon discovered, the owner gave the tours herself. Elaine Brunner described to my little group of visitors how she had bought the house in the late 1950s to rescue it from demolition, and then devoted her life to restoring it as best she could afford. In that work she had shown a great respect for John Soane, the architect who remodelled the house after a devastating fire in 1820. But the house had traces of Brunner as well as Soane. There were vases of feathers and a predominance of pink decor.

The lady herself was elderly but vigorous. She had something of the school ma'am about her. She would ask my tour group questions, and when I once gave a wrong answer, she called me a stupid boy. There was no reason for her to know it but I was a junior government minister at the time and I was no longer told off like that very often!

Years later the BBC asked me to make a short film about a piece of architecture that I loved. I thought of Wotton at once, and of Mrs Brunner. She had been an actress and when we arrived with our camera to ask her about Wotton, she gave a wonderful performance. As we were leaving, she broke all the conventions of broadcasting by addressing the lens directly to say how much she had enjoyed our visit. It made wonderful television. Her relationship with the camera reminded me of the climax of *Sunset Boulevard*, and sadly it was indeed Mrs Brunner's last public performance before her death a few months later.

Her enthusiasm for the house had infected me. To this day as I move about the house I hear her descriptions of Soane's skilful work there: how he had reduced its height to make it appear wider and grander. She pointed out how the beautiful curving staircase seems to hover in the air. Each time she climbed it past the series of arched openings she would exclaim at the lovely views down into the house. As she walked along the corridor running at the back of the house, through its fanciful arches, under the balcony bridge that introduces the secondary staircase, Mrs Brunner fancied that she was in a streetscape, maybe borrowed from Verona.

Soane found all the floors destroyed by fire and so was able at the entrance of the house to provide a magnificent open space, a tribune rising through all three floors up to a roof light. Regrettably, floors were put back early in the twentieth century. The roof light remains. As the sunlight streams into the top storey, you sense the challenge that remains. It will require enormous work if Wotton is to be fully restored to Soane's design.

Wotton's architectural magnificence inspires but does not intimidate. Its beautiful park offers a rich variety of vistas, not least back towards the house itself, and many a haven for quiet contemplation. As Mrs Brunner so remarkably demonstrated, Soane created at Wotton not a soulless hall, but a home to be lived in.

Michael Portillo on the roof of Wotton House, 1997.
Photograph: Ptolemy Dean

The Hall partly restored, only the tribune above remains to be re-opened © Paul Barker/ *Country Life* Picture Library, 2004

INTRODUCTION

DAVID GLADSTONE

When April and I inherited Wotton in 1998 the first question we had to ask ourselves was what purpose a house like Wotton can best serve in the 21st century. It ceased to be an ancestral home when the Grenville family sold it to Michael Beaumont in 1924. It ceased to function as the centre of village life when Beaumont sold the estate in 1947 and it was broken up by the Merchant Venturers of Bristol. It is not big or grand or historic enough to serve as a major visitor attraction, but its Grade I listing marks it out as an important part of the national heritage. It looks too big to serve just as a retirement home for a married couple.

In the end the question more or less answered itself. Thanks to Soane's obsession with comfort and practicality, Wotton is much more manageable than most stately homes and his guest apartments convert naturally into flats. We have found it very easy to live in the house, while making small adjustments to allow for eventual use as a film set or back-drop for fashion shoots, an exhibition space, a venue for weddings, banquets or small conferences, or a concert hall.

A more vexing question was how best to conserve it. The fact that the house's tercentenary is being celebrated in Sir John Soane's Museum is proof enough that it is now generally thought of as one of his houses. But Soane did not build Wotton and the unknown architect responsible for the original 1704 house deserves to be remembered too, together with the Grenville family who commissioned him (or her) and lived in the house for its first two centuries. There was A S G Butler, who did his best to obliterate all traces of Soane but whose 1929 make-over was in its own

Watercolour view of the garden front in 1818 drawn by John Buckler (Cat.46)

The entrance front in 1949 © *Country Life* Picture Library

The garden front in 1949 © *Country Life* Picture Library

terms thorough, coherent and executed to a high standard of workmanship. Nor could we forget the contribution of April's mother, Elaine Brunner, who saved Wotton from demolition in 1957 and stamped her formidable character on the house for the next 40 years.

The restoration programme put in hand in 1998 and now complete, apart from the Tribune and main staircase, has attempted to take account of all these factors. We have given primacy to Soane's legacy, but have preserved some of Butler's alterations and integrated them as ingeniously as we could into the Soanean setting. In the Saloon for example, Butler's Corinthian doorcases are completely at odds with Soane's rather austere conception but, since the room now hosts regular concerts, we have retained them and sought to exploit their operatic flamboyance. Butler's fine black and white marble squares in the Hall floor survive in creative tension with Soane's surrounding Painswick stone. We have retained or introduced Grenville souvenirs. And Mrs Brunner's spirit lives on in the furnishings, furniture and myriad *objets*.

For the rest, we have looked both forwards and backwards. We had to modernise the heating, wiring and plumbing. The kitchen had to be completely re-planned. But in the matter of decoration we knew that we could not improve on Soane's vision. Paint analysis, backed by ledger entries, showed that after the fire all the woodwork was grained, either light oak or satinwood, which was Soane's normal practice at the time. However, the walls in all the principal rooms were apparently papered, and since Soane seldom used wallpaper – at least on such a large scale – and since there is no mention of wallpapers in the account books in the Soane Museum, we concluded

that this part of the decoration was left to the client.

The challenge then was to devise a colour scheme that matched what Soane actually executed, where proof exists, and reflected as faithfully as possible what we believe to have been his intentions where proof is lacking.

So we started with the easy bit, graining the wood-work. Only it was not very easy, involving as it did painting techniques not much practised today and, as we soon realised, acres of doors, shutters, arches, wainscoting and even whole corridors. But Wotton is a lucky house and we found the necessary skills – in the case of one decorator dormant since far-off apprenticeship days – within a few miles of Wotton. Once launched, the graining programme has largely run itself. In fact, once our joiner had mastered Soane's joinery techniques, we found ourselves proceeding like the master himself, directing the restoration work through the equivalent of text messages: eg 'Wotton ceiling colour', 'corridor oak', 'size two triple reed'.

But we still had to decide how to decorate the walls: wallpaper or paint? We went for paint and tried to visualise a characteristic Soanean colour scheme that fitted the special character of Wotton. Dangerous ground, because nobody can know what precise colours he would have chosen. But, following extensive consultation and taking our cue from the bold architecture and traces of deep, warm colour detected in the hall and main staircase, we decided that the keynote must be drama. There could be no playing safe. So for three of the four principal rooms on the ground floor we devised a sequence of strong colours which have no exact counterpart in other Soane houses but reflect his life-long obsession with the Mediterranean and intensify the special character of each

The oculus of Soane's tribune revealed during restoration work
c. 1960

The Saloon prior to restoration

The Saloon restored © Paul Barker/ *Country Life* Picture Library, 2004

room. In the fourth, the Saloon-turned-concert-hall, we have found that an 18th-century pattern damask wallpaper best marries theatricality with relaxation and punctuates without jarring the sequence of painted colours in the rooms to either side.

Our remaining task is to restore the 'top-lit Tribune' in the hall, the centre-piece of Soane's re-design. By filling in the floors at first floor and attic level and destroying or altering all the other elements, Butler normalised the house and made it very difficult to imagine how extraordinary Soane's intricate composition of columns, arches and dome must have felt. Ptolemy Dean's illustration in this catalogue gives a good idea, but re-instating the composition and restoring faithfully the various elements will be a big challenge, not just financially but architecturally too. What we have done to date pales by comparison.

It is certainly very pleasant to live in one of Soane's houses. There is a majestic simplicity about Wotton which never fails to lift the spirits. But the grandeur is underpinned by exquisite attention to detail. The varied reed mouldings and other motifs he employed are like the letters in an alphabet of his own devising, the constituent parts of a language so coherent that every dot and comma misplaced or erased by subsequent alterations demands to be corrected. At the same time, Soane's unfailing concern for the comfort and convenience of his clients has ensured that this apparently imposing house can be cosy and intimate and also gratifyingly economical to run.

It has also been a privilege to gain access to that exclusive club of architects, connoisseurs and scholars who regard the Soane Museum as their spiritual home. It seems impossible to immerse oneself in Soane's work and world without emerging more civilised.

This focus on the house itself might suggest that the setting is secondary. For Soane it clearly was, since by lowering the house he made it less visible from strategic points in the landscape. But for everybody else, as Kate Graham's essay later in the catalogue shows, the Pleasure Grounds are aesthetically and historically an equal partner, the product of a unique collaboration between the owner's family, including his brother-in-law William Pitt (later Earl Chatham), and Capability Brown. We actually spend much more time dealing with the Grounds than the house because the scale of their neglect was so much greater.

The History of the Grenville Family at Wotton

Wotton House is inextricably linked to the Grenvilles, a Danish family who came to England with William the Conqueror. In 1208 Eustace de Grenville is recorded as holding two knights' fees at Wotton Underwood. In 1273 another Eustace de Grenville is recorded as having a house at Wotton (from which he alleged that William Coly and others had stolen some chattels). In 1343 William de Grenville, styled 'Lord of Wotton' obtained a licence from the Bishop of Lincoln to found a Chantry Chapel in the Church at Wotton (the Grenville Aisle which survives to this day.)

A few years earlier, William had married Agnes, daughter of William Wightham of Haddenham, who was to achieve local notoriety. In 1351 Thomas and William Freysel abducted this clearly most attractive 'Lady of Wotton', 'conveyed her naked into Bernwode Forest, and there and in divers places in the County of Bucks, unlawfully imprisoned her, for which offences Thomas Freysel was fined ten marks, and William five'.

For the next 350 years the Grenvilles seem to have shunned such excitement. They eventually bought the manorial rights to Wotton from the heirs of Walter Giffard and meanwhile, to quote *Country Life*, 'the family had been living quietly at Wotton, waxing in wealth and importance as sheriffs and knights of the shire'. But the building of Wotton House released pent-up energies and throughout the eighteenth century packs of young Grenvilles – known originally as 'Cobham's Cubs' – met there to plan the family's meteoric rise through the ranks of the aristocracy and to plot the downfall of their political rivals.

WOTTON HOUSE: AN OVERVIEW

DR GILES WORSLEY

Wotton had been home to Grenvilles for at least four centuries when Richard Grenville built Wotton House between 1704 and 1714. The architect is unknown, but the result, with a saloon and staircase decorated by Sir James Thornhill and carvings good enough to be attributed to Grinling Gibbons, was distinctly metropolitan in scale and ambition (see Cat.51). It must have been even more impressive before Soane took off the attic storey. The obvious comparison is with the most fashionable house of the day, Buckingham House in London, begun two years earlier for the Duke of Buckingham.

Nothing survives of the original interior, destroyed by fire in 1820, but the plan can be reconstructed from a survey in Sir John Soane's Museum (Cat.3). This shows that the planning was more complex than the exterior would suggest. The entrance hall was placed off-centre in the east façade, with the staircase occupying the same volume, as at Hanbury Hall, Worcestershire, where Thornhill also worked. To the right of the entrance hall was a single room, probably the family parlour, and in the south-west corner a small apartment with a single room, closet and backstairs. But the ambition of the house is revealed by the grand apartment that took up the rest of the ground floor, the central saloon, a large withdrawing room, a further drawing room, bedroom, closet and a second backstairs.

What drove Richard Grenville, who was not an MP and had no court connections, to build on such a scale, on a new site, so relatively late in life is uncertain. Nor is it clear where the money came from. Grenville had inherited the estate as long ago as 1666 as a boy of six, which meant that he was already 54 by the time he started to build. He would only survive completion by five years. The probable cause is ambition for his son, also named Richard. If so it worked. In about 1710 the younger Richard married Hester, sister of Sir Richard Temple of nearby Stowe. Though it could not have been anticipated at the time, it was their son, also Richard, who inherited Stowe when Temple, by then Viscount Cobham, died without children in 1749.

For the Grenvilles Lord Cobham's death was a major step forward. For Wotton it meant demotion. Stowe, by now one of the great country houses of England, became the new seat of the Grenvilles. Wotton, only 14 miles away, might well have been abandoned but the Grenvilles proved faithful to their old seat. Richard Grenville, now Earl Temple, let his brother George bring up his family there, and it was later used by successive eldest sons waiting to succeed. The first, second and third Dukes of Buckingham, as they subsequently became, all spent their early married lives at Wotton, which is thus a prime example of that under-researched subject the country house as home for the eldest son.

It was while Earl Temple, later second Duke, was living there that Wotton was gutted by fire in 1820. As the Grenvilles owned three other country houses beside Stowe and Wotton demolition might again have been a possibility. But family loyalty remained strong. Earl Temple's father, at that point Marquess of Buckingham, had spent his early married life at Wotton and in due course would be buried there. He was determined to rebuild.

Soane reconstructed the house within its original walls, though reducing the attics and the height of the first-floor windows. He tempted the Grenvilles with lavish interiors, including a double-height library, but the family insisted on keeping costs to a minimum. This was, after all, only the home of the heir-in-waiting, not the seat of the head of the family. The result is decidedly austere, but skilful in its planning (Cat.24).

Grand apartments were no longer in fashion. What contemporary entertaining required was a large dining room and drawing room, together with convenient family rooms. Soane achieved this by minor alterations within the surviving grid of internal walls. The small apartment in the south-west corner was thrown together to create a single large dining room, making a suite of three large entertaining rooms along the garden front. The family rooms opened off a new corridor running down the spine of the house. On one side of the hall was the library, conveniently placed by the new side door so visitors on business need not intrude on the house, a watercloset and stairs linking the dining room to the kitchen in the north wing. On the other side of the hall was another watercloset (convenient for guests), servants' stairs linking every floor in the house and a bedroom suite with a half-height dressing room and closet. These must have been cosy retreats in winter after the immensely tall principal rooms, and allowed space above for the lady's maid in a mezzanine.

With typical skill Soane modulated the central corridor to create a rich sequence of spaces, but his most impressive gesture was the entrance hall, which rose through two storeys to a top-lit dome to create a tribune. This was filled in during the 1920s. Indeed, when *Country Life* last wrote about Wotton in 1949 it was stated that all the Soane's work had been lost, according to the author in a fire. This is erroneous. There is no record of any such fire and when joinery and cornices added in the 1920s were removed in the 1950s Soane's decoration was discovered to be largely intact. The recent reinstatement of sympathetic colours, and in particular the regraining of the woodwork, has allowed the house to read again as a Soanean interior.

As the 3rd Duke had no son he continued to use Wotton after he succeeded in 1861, and is believed to have made improvements after he married his second wife in 1885. On the 3rd Duke's death in 1889 Stowe passed to the Duke's daughter Lady Kinloss and Wotton, with the title of Earl Temple, to the Duke's nephew William Gore-Langton. The Gore-Langtons, who had lived at Newton Park, Somerset, for over 250 years, had no need for Wotton so it was let, the traditional solution for surplus country houses. At the 1901 census it was occupied by Alfred Drake, a retired colonel, his family and 17 staff.

The lease was subsequently taken by the Hon. Hubert Beaumont, third son of the 1st Lord Allendale, who is noted as living at Wotton in the 1912 edition of *Kelly's Directory for Berkshire, Buckinghamshire and Oxfordshire*. After his death in 1922 his son Michael inherited the lease and in 1929, the year he was elected Conservative MP for Aylesbury and that his son was born, he bought the Wotton estate, including the villages of Dorton and Westcott, from Lord Temple. Though Earl Temple cited Wotton House as one of his seats along with Newton Park in *Burke's Peerage* throughout the 1920s, he never lived there.

For Wotton it was a lucky escape. Many country houses on secondary estates sold in the 1920s were demolished for lack of a purchaser. But it is often forgotten how many others were bought and extensively improved in the 1920s

and 30s, and this was the case with Wotton. With the US Stock Market soaring 1929 was a year of heady prosperity for those with American money like Beaumont, whose mother was the daughter of Michael Grace, the British end of the immensely successful American business W R Grace and Company. He also commissioned the architect A S G Butler, cousin of his great friend R A B Butler, who had just modernised nearby Boarstall Tower, to give the interiors a more early-18th-century feel, still evident in the saloon. Then on 24 October the American stock market collapsed in the Great Crash and the Beaumonts were forced to retrench, moving for a time to one of the wings.

Things had recovered by the eve of the Second World War, with the house run with a generous staff including a butler and two footmen. Wotton rode out the Second World War unaffected. Though a Canadian division was billeted in the park, the house was not requisitioned, possibly thanks to careful string-pulling by Michael Beaumont, and the family continued to live there. But problems soon emerged after the war. As a right-wing Conservative MP Beaumont was horrified by the new Socialist Britain. More urgently, post-war currency controls made it impossible to bring in money from America, cutting off the cash flow that supported Wotton. Harsh economising and moving out to a farmhouse might have saved the estate, but Beaumont had no intention of not living well.

So Wotton was put on the market and in 1947 Beaumont moved into Harristown House, Country Kildare, an elegant, substantial late-Georgian house with 700 acres, where his grandson still lives. Currency controls were not a problem in Ireland and Beaumont could indulge his hobbies of hunting and shooting, soon becoming Master of the Kildare Hunt.

Selling an estate like Wotton in 1947 was not easy and eventually it was bought by the Merchant Venturers of Bristol, who speculated extensively in land after the Second World War. The pleasure grounds were sold off in packets to farmers, with one field going right up to the garden front of the house, and much of the timber felled.

In 1949 when *Country Life* last published Wotton (using photographs taken while the Beaumonts were still in occupation) its future was uncertain. There was no market for private purchasers of country houses as there had been in the 1920s. One wing was sold off separately. (It was subsequently owned by Sir Arthur Bryant and Sir John Gielgud.) For a time Wotton was let to a boy's boarding school, Wotton House Boys. But that closed suddenly in

1953 and the house was left empty. It was eventually bought by Buckinghamshire County Council, who were preparing it for demolition when Elaine Brunner stepped in.

For Mrs Brunner, who was someone with the ability to fill a large space, Wotton was a challenge she could not resist. Her husband, the grandson of Sir John Brunner, founder of Brunner-Mond, one of the constituent parts of ICI, was not so keen and used to refer to the house as a 'barracks'. Wotton was bought for £6,000, payable in instalments and, advised by Robin Fedden, an old family friend, Mrs Brunner engaged the young Donald Insall to restore the house with one of the very first grants, £40,000, from the Historic Buildings Commission. This work included the removal of Butler's later embellishments, except in the saloon. Surplus rooms were discreetly divided into flats and let.

By July 1961 when Elaine Brunner's daughter April married David Gladstone the restoration of the house was largely complete. There remained the pleasure grounds, laid out around two great lakes on a scale that rivals Stowe, though with fewer, and much less elaborate, garden buildings. Piece by piece this was reassembled during the 1960s and early 1970s, though one critical field between the house and the lake was not acquired until the 1980s. A final burst of energy in the late 1980s and early 1990s saw the start of the restoration of the garden buildings, largely the work of Michael Harrison, now the estate manager.

Elaine Brunner died in 1998 and since then Mr and Mrs Gladstone have continued her work. Together, one major room a year, they have worked their way through the house, recovering the richer Soanean colours. Meanwhile, the landscape has been progressively opened up and more of the garden buildings restored. All that is left is the possible restoration of the tribune.

A longer version of this essay first appeared in Country Life,
13 May 2004

© *Country Life, 2004*

The house as found by Elaine Brunner in 1958

THE SAVING OF WOTTON IN THE FIFTIES AND SIXTIES

DONALD INSALL CBE

It was Elaine Brunner who was the saviour of Wotton. Without her imagination and persuasive organising ability, the house would have been lost. She contacted us in 1957 as architects specialising in restoration and repair work, and invited us to visit. It was a wonderful opportunity, and a huge challenge.

Elaine had recently visited Wotton with what she darkly described as 'an amorous demolition contractor', with whom she had intended negotiating for some columns or some statuary. She had become completely possessed by the pathetic sight of such a glamorous and beautiful house in such distress, and had instantly determined to set her mind to saving it.

Firstly, there were the forecourt railings and great gates. It was rumoured these were destined now for London, as a handsome screen for Holland Park House. This project was to be stopped, and stopped it was. We researched the records of the house, by this time a sad hulk, and found out about Soane's first visit in 1820, which everyone seemed to have forgotten. Like Elaine, he had arrived at a sorry moment, but on that occasion the ruins were still smoking from the devastating fire. With superb ingenuity, possibly as a financial saving, he had proposed a lowering of the attic floor across the head of the first floor windows, introducing new windows actually within the entablature of the cornice, lowering the chimneys and installing a low pitched copper roof.

The roof as we found it had evidently been relaid in over-large copper sheets, which had expanded, contracted and cracked in the sunshine, allowing major water penetration into the house. This in turn had set up dry rot, notably in massive window lintels and wall-plates, many of them buried deep in the walling and quite inaccessible. The interiors of the house were soaked, and a minor lake filled the middle of the Saloon.

As we grew more familiar with the house, it became apparent that there were three main phases – the original work, the Soane rebuilding and then a later extensive recasting by country-house architect A S G Butler. This last work now masked and concealed much work of interest by Soane. The Entrance Hall, and the central Corridor, in particular, had lost most of their meaning. But fascinating details emerged and could be rescued. Elaine developed a fine instinct for anything which savoured of Soane, but financial priorities entirely prevented any further progress whatever, except to save all we could, including opening up surviving traces behind the work of the unfortunate Butler. Thus, missing details of the Hall ceiling were restored, but without any possibility of exploring and opening up the earlier Tribune. An artist friend of the family contributed mural paintings which the future may not wish to save, and we tried to emphasise and express in all we did, the surviving Soane details. At roof construction level, evidence of the 'eye' of the Tribune was, for example, perfectly rescuable and was saved, although it could not be reopened.

Finances were a fearsome problem, and Wotton must

The owner provides personal supervision and encouragement

Patrick and Elaine relaxing from their labours

have been one of the first country houses to be assisted by the recently established Historic Buildings Council, who visited early and kept in touch through their architect Alfie Baker (second son of the great Sir Herbert). I forget whether I was yet a member of that gorgeous club of enthusiasts and mixed characters alongside inspiring members such as Nikolaus Pevsner and John Betjeman. If I was, perhaps that helped. Certainly the work could not have been achieved without their technical and financial support.

Everyone agreed to the delayed reduction of the chimneys, as proposed by Soane but not executed, then too perhaps on grounds of economy. Now they were in poor shape and still presented a strange skyline above the otherwise lowered silhouette.

The exercise was teamwork, and all Elaine's friends were meanwhile drawn into it. An interior decorator friend, Baroness Diana Pirquet, was charmed into accepting the use of the similarly derelict North Pavilion for her own lifetime, and in consideration of similarly rescuing it. Crowned with a clock-turret, this had been the Kitchen

pavilion, serving along a basement dog-leg link-corridor whose original floor-level we rediscovered, realising it had also been raised to a more practical level, by a brick addition along the top of its oval-windowed stone base.

There was a basement Orangery looking south over gardens here, but similarly wrecked. And adjoining it, the South Pavilion which with its extra basement floor had more accommodation. This had been sold separately and was the home of Sir Arthur Bryant, regular weekly contributor to *Country Life*. We understood he always knew just how long to write, and never needed to recheck his fluent dictated comments. On his death Elaine succeeded in attracting the interest of fellow-thespian Sir John Gielgud who came to live there.

Elaine's bearded husband Patrick, ex-RAF, took an immense daily interest. A boating enthusiast, it was he who insisted and persuaded the HBC's architect upon his idea of replacing the external cornice not in woodwork, which could well have instantly become lost to the dry rot from timbers inside the walling, but in impervious fibreglass.

A meeting on site, watched with interest by Elaine's recycled statues

A less than watertight roof

This was in the spirit of experiment, but he was determined it should be done, and Elaine agreed. The result seems to have been remarkably satisfactory, and being self-coloured, the cornice has had no need of painting. The acorn pendants are all reinstated originals. That the change of materials was acceptable to the Ministry and the HBC was once again, a triumph of the charms and persuasions of the redoubtable Elaine. Meanwhile, she was actively and indeed aggressively negotiating for the repurchase of lost land, scouring and draining the lake and pursuing every possible opportunity of reinstating Wotton. Peter Locke and I as her architects visited regularly, staying into the evenings and dining with her and her dogs, returning down the drive by the light of our ancient Rolls Royce's head-lamps just short of midnight. Sometimes too, Elaine would drive Patrick's Jaguar XK140 to show us their other house at Beaconsfield. She rarely advanced beyond third gear, but it was all part of the excitement. Everyone was in thrall to her energetic leadership. There were tragedies as well as joys – the long-suffering builder employed a foreman who one day was mixing lime in the basement which exploded and in the enclosed space entered his eye. Although he was rushed to hospital, he sadly lost his sight. On another occasion, over-enthusiastic scaffolders lost control of a metal pole which penetrated the house and shattered a small marble table near which our client had been sitting.

The whole exercise was an extraordinary experience. Perhaps the greatest joy was the splendid and delightful occasion of the wedding to David Gladstone of Elaine's daughter April. We are friends to this day, and were the architects for their London house in Islington. Whether it is a Buckingham or a Soane, or a Brunner or a Gladstone, it is each generation's very special people who combine to settle the fate of a country's greatest houses.

THE PLEASURE GROUNDS AT WOTTON

KATE GRAHAM

'When a little rustling of birds in the spray, the leaping of fish, and the fragrancy of the woodbine, denote the approach of the evening; while the setting sun shoots its last gleams on a Tuscan portico, which is close to the upper basin, but which from a seat near this river is seen at a distance, through all the obscurity of the wood, glowing on the banks, and reflected on the surface of the water.'

Thomas Whateley, *Observations on Modern Gardening*, 1771 (on Wotton)

Wotton's gardens, once famous enough to attract visitors like Whateley from far and wide, began life in 1704 when Richard Grenville instructed George London and Henry Wise (two of the most important English landscape designers of their time) to create a suitably splendid garden for the newly constructed Wotton House. Their work, fairly typical of the period, consisted largely of constructing a ha-ha (a ditch with retaining wall used to divide land without disrupting the landscape), and an ornamental flower garden or *parterre* to the west of the house. In addition, several grand avenues were planted in the gardens and the wider park. These improvements set the pattern for the development of the gardens for the rest of the 18th century, as seen in the 1789 plan of the pleasure grounds.[1]

Although relatively little is known about the changes made to the gardens during the 18th century, it is evident that its latter half saw much activity and change within the landscape. It seems that the most significant changes were carried out by Lancelot 'Capability' Brown (1716–83) under the direction of the owner George Grenville (1712–70)

Watercolour view of the garden front in 1816 drawn by John Buckler and featured in Lysons' *History of Buckinghamshire* (Cat.50)

The Ionic building on Grotto Island as illustrated in the Lysons volume

and his brother-in-law William Pitt the Elder (1708–78). Written evidence for these changes is scarce but it is clear from 18th-century account books that Brown was at Wotton in the 1740s, 1750s and again in the late 1760s. It is difficult to be specific about his work but his fingerprints can be seen in the archaeology of the landscape: in the shaping of the Warrells and the design of the larger lake and the connecting serpentine rivers; planting that through colour and form highlighted aspects of the landscape; carefully planned vistas and the use of bridges and other garden buildings to complement the design, all features typical of a Brownian landscape.

The concurrent development of the gardens at Stowe, the other seat of the Grenville family, must also have exerted an influence at Wotton. We know, for example, that the Chinese House that stood on China Island at Wotton for nearly 200 years was brought from Stowe in the 1750s, and that the design of the Five Arch Bridge was influenced by Kent's Shell Bridge at Stowe. Yet, while Stowe's buildings were grand exemplars of work from the best architects and craftsmen, the garden buildings at Wotton were simpler affairs and mostly constructed in wood.

The improvement of the grounds became one of George Grenville's passions and also drew the enthusiasm of his friend and eventual brother-in-law William Pitt. Their interest was an indication of the degree to which the family were involved in shaping the landscape – even George Grenville's wife Elizabeth can lay claim to the title of architect of one of the garden buildings. In 1758 she wrote to the architect Sanderson Miller (1717–80)[2] asking his approval of her design for a building with 'Ionick Pillars'[3] for Grotto Island.

Thomas Beade's 1789 plan of the pleasure grounds depicts the main features of the 18th-century landscape which, apart from when affected by the gradual process of decay, remained essentially unaltered in form until the mid-20th century. There were approximately twelve garden buildings on the circuit including Elizabeth's grotto (the Malay Hut was one of the few 18th-century additions). One hundred and fifty years later, only seven of these remained and in various states of repair. The gardens were also rich in statuary including a Neptune, a Mars and a Jupiter. No traces of these classically inspired sculptures remain although the owners have since installed a Venus where Jupiter once stood in a leafy glade along the southern length of the circuit.

By the time Soane arrived at Wotton in 1820, the gardens had changed little since George Grenville's day. Soane's restoration of the house after the 1820 fire had no direct impact on the gardens, but the lowering of the attic storey and the rebuilding of the nine chimneystacks altered the appearance of the building. Although Soane did not change the position of the house he would certainly have hoped that its more refined and 'classical' appearance would enrich the views from within the gardens and across the wider park.

When the late Elaine Brunner rescued the house from demolition in the 1950s, she understood that the house and landscape were inextricably linked and that any restoration project would have to include the pleasure grounds. At that time the gardens were sub-divided, having been sold off to neighbouring farms, and those garden buildings which had not disappeared completely were dangerously dilapidated. The 18th-century Palladian and Crescent Bridges had vanished and the Rotunda, the Turkish Tent and Tuscan Pavilions were all in desperate need of repair. The historic

The Tuscan Pavilions

View over the Lake from the Doric Temple

planting had become confused and overgrown and the general meaning of the grand landscape design had been eroded and lost in part.

The restoration of the gardens initiated by Mrs Brunner and continued by her daughter and son-in-law cannot create a facsimile of the great Grenville landscape but what is clear is that as each acre of ground is recovered and replanted, and each building restored, a little more of the magic is returning. Reinstating the connection between landscape and architecture is at the heart of Wotton's recovery and involves restoring the original design concept and reuniting its various elements. The replanting of avenues, the recovery of earth and waterworks and the repair and reconstruction of garden buildings are all part of the process of recreating the 'greatness of unity' that Whateley speaks of elsewhere in his account of the gardens.

The Palladian and Crescent Bridges have both now been reconstructed. Simple in design but faithful to their predecessors, the new bridges help to make sense of the 18th-century garden circuit. Similarly, the repair of Five Arch Bridge has added to our understanding of how the buildings were sometimes used to trick the eye, in this case acting as a disguise for the change in levels of two associated bodies of water.

The repair and reconstruction of the other garden buildings has also been integral to the recovery of the original design concept. The Turkish Tent, restored in the early 1990s and again in recent years, is one of the most important buildings in the gardens because of its position within the landscape and the sight lines that extend from it. From the three 'windows' of the Tent the formal relationship between the Rotunda (at the centre), the Poplar Urn (to the north) and the Grotto (to the south) can be observed,

creating three perfectly framed painted landscapes. Such vignettes were an 18th-century ideal of landscape gardening. Horace Walpole (1717–97) wrote frequently of such scenes claiming that '. . . this country exhibits the most beautiful landscapes in the world when they are framed . . .'[4]

At Wotton today, the qualities that charmed Whateley are palpable in the atmosphere. However, this pleasing sense of continuity conceals the fact that the pleasure grounds that Whateley visited, and that were nurtured and developed by several generations of the Grenville family, suffered many years of decline and only narrowly escaped total destruction in the mid-20th century. The on-going restoration of the gardens has already partly recreated Whateley's experience of visiting 'a spot so rich as this in beauties peculiar to its character'. There is more work to be done, and much important archival material waiting to be unearthed across the Atlantic,[5] but through the commitment and interest of the current owners, the gardens are coming back to life. Although George Grenville might not recognise his pleasure grounds in their maturity, he would undoubtedly take pride in their endurance and recovery.

1   Thomas Beade, *A Plan of the Marquess of Buckingham's Seat and Pleasure Ground at Wotton in the County of Bucks. Surveyed 1789*, British Library Maps 1580.
2   Sanderson Miller is known to have designed at least two buildings in the garden: the Octagon (Warwickshire County Record Office CR125/B601) and a bridge, probably Five Arch Bridge (ibid CR125/B601).
3   '. . . Grotto upon the new island with Ionick pillars . . . decorated with shells and the pillars with flints and shells like some that are at Stowe' (ibid CR125/B587).
4   The Yale edition of Horace Walpole's correspondence, Volume 35, p.282: letter to Horace Walpole the Younger, 26 June 1792.
5   The Grenville family papers were purchased in 1925 by the Huntingdon Library in San Marino, California, following the Stowe sale in 1921.

The garden front under restoration *c.* 1960

WOTTON IN CONTEXT

PETER INSKIP

To understand the rebuilding of Wotton in 1820, one needs to appreciate not only the way it fits in with the large body of work carried out by Soane for the Grenvilles, but also the family's passion for architecture that was demonstrated throughout the preceding century.

It is clear that Richard Grenville wanted a decidedly smart, up-to-date seat when he commissioned a new house on his ancestral estate at Wotton in 1704. The master mason was John Keene, the architect is unknown, but a topographical sketch of the entrance court exists by Sir James Thornhill. The design followed the pattern of Buckingham House in St James's Park with the main body connected by discreet quadrants to visually free-standing pavilions that housed kitchens and stables. Buckingham House had been built in 1702–05 to the designs of either William Winde or John Talman; it immediately became one of the most imitated houses in England. However, whilst other copies such as Cound (1704), Chicheley (1719), and even Cottesbrooke (1702–13) were variants, the detail and arrangement of Wotton remained very close to its model. That such a spectacular, modern house, constructed with the best London craftsmen, should have been built by an ancient gentry family must have also reflected its social ambitions.

Wotton was nearing completion when Richard Grenville's son married Hester Temple in 1710. She was the daughter of a neighbour, Sir Richard Temple of Stowe, and he also had been responsible for completely rebuilding his own family seat. Soon after her husband inherited Wotton in 1719, her brother, Viscount Cobham, started the development of Stowe and its landscape on a palatial scale. When he died childless in 1749, it was arranged that Mrs Grenville succeeded to her brother's honours and properties with the titles of Viscontess Cobham and Countess Temple; and thus Wotton became the second house on the combined estates. Her son, Richard Grenville, had been groomed as Lord Cobham's heir for some years and he became 2nd Earl Temple on the death of his mother in 1752. Before his uncle's death he had already become deeply involved with the architectural work at Stowe, particularly with the Grecian Temple which was being constructed under the direction of Capability Brown in 1747, possibly to a design by James Gibbs. The temple was roofed-in by 1749, but underwent almost immediate modification under Borra to render it truly 'Grecian'; with further embellishments it was rededicated as the Temple of Concord and Victory in 1763. A portrait by Hoare of 1760 depicting Lord Temple holding a plan of the Grecian Building characterises the family's deep interest in its architectural projects.

The architectural patronage of the family can be seen in three distinct phases: Lord Cobham had used only the best architects available, and this had resulted in making Stowe an architectural treasury of the work of Vanbrugh, Gibbs and Kent by the time of his death. In contrast, under Lord Temple, there was a shift in patronage and amateur enthusiasm, aided by less talented professionals, was to prevail at Stowe as well as at Wotton where a series of garden monuments was also constructed. However, from 1765, Lord Temple was ably supported by his cousin, Thomas Pitt, who designed the monumental Corinthian Arch at Stowe and realised Robert Adam's scheme of 1770 for recasting the South Front of the mansion, after the architect had withdrawn as it appears that he could not tolerate the Earl's incessant meddling with his proposals. The final flowering of the family's passion for architecture was the patronage of Sir John Soane under Earl Temple's nephew, George Grenville, 1st Marquess of Buckingham and his son, Richard Grenville, 2nd Marquess, who was created 1st Duke of Buckingham and Chandos in 1822. During their time, Soane was loyally consulted for a period of more than thirty years.

It must have been Thomas Pitt who introduced John Soane to his cousin. He had befriended him in Italy in 1778 and he had already recommended the architect to another cousin, William Pitt 'the younger', who sought advice about his house at Holwood in Kent in 1786.[1] Despite Soane's reputed denial, the commission from the Prime Minister must have helped to secure his appointment as Surveyor to

Fig.1. Elevation of Buckingham House, Pall Mall. Royal Academy Lecture drawing

the Bank of England two years later. Soane's greatest work for the 1st Marquess was the creation of Buckingham House, Pall Mall in 1790;[2] for his son, it was the rebuilding of Wotton in 1820. They proved to be his first and last commissions for the family.

The Crown lease of No.91 Pall Mall was associated with Wotton as it was a Grenville property by 1737. However, for fifty years, only minor alterations were carried out, possibly because of Lord Temple's preoccupation with finishing his uncle's great house and garden. It was only after his death in 1779 and the completion of Stowe House, that the family turned its attention to Pall Mall. In 1781, the 1st Marquess purchased the lease of the adjoining house and 'laid the said two Messuages together'.[3] This was affected by some minor alterations by R F Brettingham, who had worked for him at No.9 Berkeley Square before he had inherited. The enlarged house, however, proved unsatisfactory.

Soane developed his scheme from March 1790[4] and the house was completed in 1795. The whole project was carried out with many hours of close consultation with his client and the architect noted that 'Since no departures were made from the original designs and he had been allowed to carry out his architectural intentions fully, the estimates were completely accurate.'[5] Soane replaced the western house with a totally new structure. Elements of that on the east were retained and provided the cue for the disposition of the windows in the severe neo-classical façade (Fig.1) with which he re-fronted the whole property. Typical of London houses, the plain front concealed the elaborate interior that was needed for lavish entertaining.

The stair, brilliantly inserted across the core of the original house, was the key to the design. By extending

Fig.2. Perspective View of the Staircase, Buckingham House. Royal Academy Lecture drawing

the bottom three steps to the full width of the stair hall, Soane exploited the change of level between the two buildings, using it to demarcate the transition between the private rooms on the east side of the ground floor and the public rooms on the west. However, it was the overall spatial organisation that was so remarkable, with its progression from an oval entrance hall via a lozenge-shaped stair compartment to the principal reception rooms on the first floor. In addition, the progressive opening up of the volume of the staircase gave an impression of space extending on all four sides of the attic storey set beneath a glazed lantern (Fig.2). Thus, it represents an early stage in Soane's systematic development of the theme of the top-lit tribune and, of course, it anticipates his various proposals thirty years later for the entrance hall at Wotton.

The acquisition of new commissions by Soane was not always easy. It must have been a disappointment when the Marquess's younger brother employed Samuel Wyatt in 1792 to design Dropmore House, and especially so as Lord Grenville had married the daughter of his mentor, Thomas Pitt. At about this time, Soane was also attempting to secure the commission for rebuilding the House of Lords. However, George III thought that it should be Gothic and James Wyatt was eventually appointed. Soane was bitterly

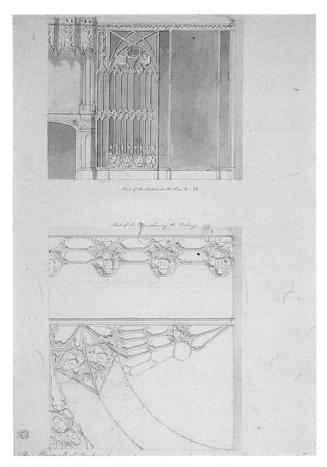

Fig.3. Design for part of the Gothic Library at Stowe, 15 March 1805

disappointed and had expected Buckingham's support, but there was silence. The Marquess eventually wrote that he had no voice in the matter, but he admitted that he favoured a Gothic solution where the new House of Lords fronted Westminster Abbey, though he was 'not sure whether I should not have preserved a grecian front to the River'. Soane scribbled on the letter: 'So much for Buckingham!'[6]

Despite these upsets, the architect's involvement with the Grenvilles continued and his Gothic Library of 1805–7 is one of the best rooms at Stowe (Fig.3).[7] A repository was needed for the newly acquired collections of early English or 'Saxon' manuscripts which had been left to the Marquess by Thomas Astle in 1803. Space was adapted in the basement storey below the main library and was intended to contain a shrine with a portrait of the bene-factor in a recess opposite the chimney-piece. In concept, therefore, the Gothic Library anticipated the Dulwich Picture Gallery with its central mausoleum.

It was expressly stipulated by Soane's client that his new library should be Gothic, and the Marquess suggested that he should take advice on the 'various Gothicks'

from the antiquary John Carter.[8] The space, however, was entirely Soane's: the shallowest of vaults hovered over the bookcases, lead castings formed the intricate canopies over the doors, crimson velvet panels above both the fireplace and the shrine provided the background for the display of antique jewels; and the polished brass chimney-piece was complemented by ebonised furniture inlaid with ivory quatrefoils. At the centre of the ceiling, a painted display of arms proclaimed the ancestry and connections of the Grenvilles, heralding that introduced in the hall at Wotton fifteen years later. Typical of the architect's work nearly everything was constructed and decorated by his trusted London craftsmen.

Soane's involvement with the 1st Marquess also led to work in Oxford. Buckingham had already endowed Brasenose College with a number of new fellowships since the Principal had been the tutor at Stowe. Despite the experience of the Gothic Library and the fact that Soane was working in that style at Ramsey Abbey, his proposals of 1807 for substantial additions were offered only in Roman and Greek forms (Fig.4).[9] None of the schemes was realised, but the sunk mouldings on the door and window joinery are surviving evidence that minor alterations were carried out.[10]

Following in the steps of Earl Temple, it is clear that Soane's patron sometimes played an active part in the design process himself and this is confirmed in the architect's ninth Lecture to the Royal Academy, delivered in 1815:

> General convenience in buildings for domestic purposes must . . . always take the lead, and certainly in most cases we shall be justified in sacrificing magnificence and even appearance to convenience. But that both may be obtained, and the grandeur of the entrance

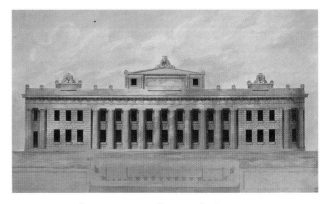

Fig. 4. Design for Brasenose College, Oxford

Fig.5. Egyptian Hall or Winter Entrance at Stowe House, looking west by John Claude Nattes, 1805. Stowe School Archives

Fig.6. The avenue lodges and view of Buckingham Church by John Claude Nattes, 1809. From the Buckinghamshire County Museum collections

preserved, has lately been shown in the north entrance into Stowe House. For this noble conception the lovers of architecture are indebted to the late Marquess of Buckingham, whose taste and skill in designing can only be equalled by the other distinguished talents which that noble encourager of the fine arts so pre-eminently possessed.[11]

The Winter Entrance was introduced at Stowe soon after the turn of the century. Flanking balustrades conceal carriage ramps that descend to a *porte-cochère* that was cut in beneath the existing Ionic portico and led direct to a new hall at basement level, whence a tight staircase rose to William Kent's main entrance hall above on the *piano nobile*. It was described as the Egyptian Hall by 1805 (Fig.5) and, given that it was under construction in 1803,[12] the design must count as one of the earliest extant examples of full-blooded Egyptian revival architecture.[13] Although some of the details might not be sophisticated enough in their design or execution for attribution to Soane, it is difficult to imagine that the arrangement of the west end, with its stove designed as a sarcophagus set behind a screen carrying funereal urns, was not directly influenced by him. However, Soane confirms that this was not his work, and one has to accept it as a homage to him by the Marquess. It is likely that other unattributed structures at Stowe dating from this period had a similar genesis: the monumentality of the Buckingham Lodges is reinforced at each corner by strigulated, Coade stone altars that could be characteristic of Soane, but the overall design is again less assured (Fig.6).

Following the succession of the 2nd Marquess in 1813, Soane was preparing schemes for rebuilding the laundry wing of Stowe[14] as a self-contained, private family apartment. It would have brought a delightful informality to Stowe with its close relationship to the Flower Garden. The proposals of 1817 are also interesting as they demonstrate the continuing involvement of the family in the design process. Soane's plan is inscribed as 'from a sketch by Lady Grenville', the Marquess's aunt and, as mentioned above, the daughter of Thomas Pitt. His scheme closely follows her drawing that survives amongst his own plans. Soane's primary contribution appears to have been the highly original elevations. If the scheme had been built, the adoption of the gigantic rusticated basement from the South Front coupled with the domestic scale of Vanbrugh's service building that existed on the site would have ensured an appropriate status for the new wing without disrupting the architectural hierarchies of the mansion.

The Gothic Cross at Stowe also dates from this period (Fig.7). It was one of the most ambitious bespoke productions of Coade, whose account for the 'Rich Gothic

Fig. 7. Gothic cross at Stowe, 1827. Engraving. Victoria and Albert Museum. Photo: M.J. Bevington

Fig.8. Antique gemstones acquired by Sir John Soane from the Duke of Buckingham in 1834

Monument or Cross with pinnacles' at a cost of 200 guineas was submitted in 1815.[15] The tiered arrangement of the monument and the views through its open arches have parallels in various constructions in the courtyards behind No.13 Lincoln's Inn Fields, and Soane's frequent collaborations with Mrs Coade as well as the loyalty of the Grenvilles to their architect would make it surprising if he had no connection with the monument. What is more, between 1813 and 1814, Soane was remodelling the Library and Dressing Room at Buckingham House[16] and it would have been strange if the subject of the proposed cross had not been raised in their discussions.

The 2nd Marquess also involved Soane with other properties. In 1810, he had bought Sudeley Castle, Gloucestershire as it was the ancestral home of his wife's family, having been granted to the Brydges, later Dukes of Chandos, in 1554. Slighted in 1649, it was probably completely uninhabitable by the time of the purchase. Soane started to prepare designs for rebuilding in 1819,[17] but nothing came of it and the estate was disposed of in 1837.

The most likely reason that the rehabilitation of Sudeley Castle did not proceed is that events were overtaken by the disastrous fire that gutted Wotton House in October 1820. This time, the building was the historic seat of the Grenvilles themselves and their final resting place remained securely within Wotton church and not at Stowe. Wotton had been the Marquess's home before he succeeded his father and the house was held with filial piety. At once, an urgent note was despatched to Soane 'I beg to see you immediately without a moment's loss of time. Poor Wotton is burned down.'[18]

Soane's designs for rebuilding the house were soon ready. Like his father, the 2nd Marquess seems to have been essentially conservative. At first glance, it appears that the architect followed his client's instruction that the house was to keep close to the appearance of the original exterior, but his drawing of the entrance elevation demonstrates the degree to which he subtly remodelled it to something far more elegant, reducing the house visually from three storeys to two. Inside, a completely new interior was inserted within the discipline of the main walls that survived the fire, but his principal alteration to the fabric was the conversion of the modest hall into a lofty tribune that cut through the two storeys above and terminated with a circular dome carrying a glazed lantern. Despite initial hesitations, his client could not have been more delighted with the completed house and wrote 'your plan and execution of it are perfect and beautiful. You have restored to life my old mansion.'[19] In reality, Soane had totally transformed what had become a very old fashioned, Queen Anne mansion into a very personal work of his own.

By the late 1820s, the 1st Duke, as the Marquess had by then been elevated, found himself in serious economic problems and in 1833 he turned to Soane to assist him with a loan of £5,000 on the score of longstanding friendship. It was all part of the collapse of the Grenvilles' fortunes and anticipated the financial ruin of his son, the 2nd Duke, which resulted in the sale of the contents of Stowe in 1848. Today, such an approach to an architect might seem strange, but with Soane supported by a lucrative practice and a substantial inheritance via his wife there are several instances of his acting as a banker to other clients with whom he had developed close friendships at about this time.[20] At Stowe, however, he declined the Duke's request, but instead offered to purchase for his own collection illuminated manuscripts and antique gems[21] which the Duke had recently acquired and which were then housed in the Gothic Library. The pieces were brought down to London where Soane viewed them at Buckingham House. The acquisition in 1833 at a cost of seven hundred guineas of Cardinal Marino Grimani's Commentary on the Epistle of St Paul to the Romans, together with three other Renais-sance copies of the Book of Hours, and the purchase, in the following year, of two hundred and seventy five 'antique' Roman gemstones at a cost of £1,000, marked the end of the imaginative architectural patronage of the Grenvilles that had spanned five generations (Fig.8).

1   Soane worked at Holwood, Kent, for William Pitt the Younger in 1786 and again in 1796–99 when he designed the Library. See SM drawings, drawer 2, set 9.

2   Buckingham House, then the Old War Office, was demolished in 1907 to make way for the Royal Automobile Club.

3   F H W Sheppard (ed.), *Survey of London vol. XXIX–XXX, The Parish of St James Westminster, Part One: South of Piccadilly*, London, 1960, p. 360, note 134, quotes Public Record Office LRR 063/82, pp. 85–90.

4   SM drawings, drawer 33, set 1.

5   Sir John Soane, *Memoirs of the Professional Life of an Architect*, London, 1835, p.24.

6   Arthur T. Bolton (ed.), *The Portrait of Sir John Soane, RA, (1753–1837), set forth in Letters from his Friends (1775–1837)*, London, 1927, p. 89.

7   SM drawings, drawer 33, set 3; Henry Huntington Library: Stowe Maps and Plans, Box 9, Willis 7 also contains drawings of panelling for the Gothic Library and Vestibule.

8   Gillian Darley, *John Soane: An Accidental Romantic*, New Haven and London, 1999, p. 163.

9   SM drawings, drawer 33, set 4, 1804–1808.

10 Ptolemy Dean kindly drew my attention to the Soanian details that he has identified in the college.

11 David Watkin, *Sir John Soane: Enlightenment Thought and the Royal Academy lectures*, Cambridge, 1996, p. 619; quotes RA Lectures, Second Series, Lecture IX, 2 March 1815.

12 Henry Huntington Library: Stowe Garden Accounts, box 14, bundle 8.

13 Nattes prepared two views of the Egyptian Hall. That looking west is now in the possession of Stowe School; that looking east belongs to the Buckinghamshire County Museum, Aylesbury.

14 SM drawings, drawer 33, set 2.

15 Henry Huntington Library: Stowe Garden Accounts, Repairs box 116, bundle 16.

16 SM drawings, drawer 33, set 1.

17 SM drawings, drawer 33, set 3, 1819.

18 Ptolemy Dean, *Sir John Soane and the Country Estate*, London, 1999, p.161, fig. 11.17 quotes SM Priv. Corr. XIII.C.2.17.

19 Darley, op.cit., p. 263, quotes SM Priv. Corr.XIII.C.3.27, 9 Nov 1823.

20 Soane lent Stephen Thornton, a friend and director of the Bank of England, as well as a long standing client for whom he had recast Moggerhanger House, Bedfordshire, in 1810, the sum of £500 at an interest of 5 per cent per annum in 1833. It is noted that, whilst the interest rate was the same, the capital was only a tenth of that requested by the Duke of Buckingham.

21 Peter Thornton and Helen Dorey, *A Miscellany of Objects from Sir John Soane's Museum*, London, 1992, pp. 56, 103.

A longer version of this essay first appeared in Apollo, *April 2004*

© *Apollo, 2004*

SOANE AT WOTTON

WILLIAM PALIN

The story of the devastating fire at Wotton in October 1820 and John Soane's subsequent involvement in the restoration of the house has been recounted in a number of books and articles, most recently, and comprehensively in Ptolemy Dean's *John Soane and the Country Estate*.[1] However, this exhibition marks the first time the key drawings have been displayed together, allowing us to follow the story of this fascinating project through the eyes of the architect. These drawings provide an insight into Soane's creative process and, together with the supporting documentation,[2] reveal his struggle to reconcile the demands of the client with his own grand architectural visions. Soane was in his late sixties when he took on the project but his zest for architecture was evidently undimmed. His arrival at the house two days after the fire marked the first of 18 visits. There are over 100 entries in Soane's office Day Books relating to the house and 50 drawings survive.

The necessary information for Soane's redesign was gathered by his Clerk of Works, James Cook, who was dispatched to the stricken house within hours of Buckingham's desperate letter (Cat.33). A group of what can loosely be described as survey drawings show the house in its ruined state, the most dramatic of these depicting the interior of the burned out shell (Fig.1) complete with jagged cracks in the brick walls. The drawing of the entrance front

has been tidied up to give an impression of the pre-fire house, complete with the full complement of nine chimneystacks. It is clear from the outset that Soane intended to lower the imposing 1700s façade to give the house a broader more classical outline, and on a drawing for the garden front, which belongs to this early group, he introduces his new, lowered design on the right-hand side.

Soane had two clients at Wotton, Lord Buckingham, the owner, and his son Lord Grenville, the occupier.[3] From the start it was Buckingham who assumed the more active role, with Grenville consulted only after his father had scrutinised the designs. Negotiations between Soane and his Wotton clients are distinguished from the outset by strong sense of urgency and a concern for economy. Soane had worked on a number of projects for Buckingham's father (see pp.22–27) and the Marquess knew that efficiency was one of this architect's most valuable assets. True to form, just a week after the fire Soane was ready with his new designs. The two men met, appropriately, at the house in Pall Mall Soane had designed for the 1st Marquess some thirty years before.[4] Soane presented his client with six drawings including a part elevation of the entrance front showing the proposed lowering of the upper two storeys.

The following day Soane's office produced a neat plan of the ground storey. This plan shows the position of the

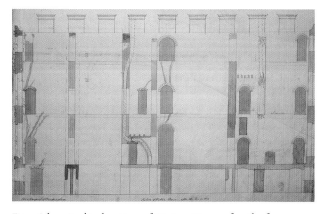

Fig.1. A longitudinal section of Wotton House after the fire, drawn by James Cook, showing the cracks in the skeleton of the building (Cat.2)

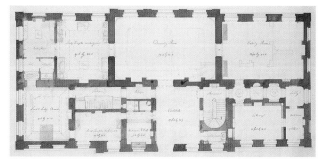

Fig.2. The first arrangement of ground floor rooms as proposed by Soane, introducing a new axis of symmetry (SM 34/1/16)

north-south corridor, the Vestibule and the two main staircases (Fig.2) and sets the basic pattern for the final designs. Comparing this plan to the survey drawing of the old house (Fig.3) the direction of Soane's thinking is clear. The pre-fire plan was basically a series of interconnecting spaces, the structural skeleton of which had to be retained to avoid rocketing costs. Soane transforms this old-fashioned arrangement by adding an independent spine corridor running the full length of the house. This passageway is achieved by the introduction of just one new opening. Another north-south axis is introduced by centring the doorways between the rooms on the west side. Soane's other changes are dictated by practical concerns. His Wotton would be a modern house with multiple circulation routes, the latest services and well-heated rooms to satisfy the demands of modern living. Thus on the new plan certain windows are blocked to allow the introduction of additional fireplaces (Fig.4) and water closets appear. A

secondary staircase serving all four floors is integrated into the corridor. Soane would later introduce a third staircase by the side entrance leading from the basement up to a WC. Later still he would add a staircase on the third floor to give access to the attic at the northern end of the house (Fig.5).

The plans were refined further during an eventful follow-up meeting with Buckingham at Stowe on 17 November,[5] by which time Soane had prepared some larger plans, and also perspective views of the new Hall and Library.[6] Buckingham's direct involvement in the project is revealed by his pencil annotations to the plans (Fig.6).[7] He moves the private apartments from the ground to the first floor (allowing the completion of a suite of three large rooms on the ground floor) and rejects Soane's grand double-height library on the ground floor. Perhaps the most interesting alteration is the addition of an entrance at the side of the house providing direct access to the north-south corridor.

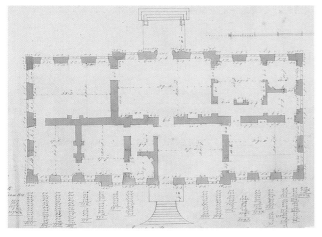

Fig.3. Survey drawing of the ground floor prior to Soane's restoration, measured by James Cook (Cat.3)

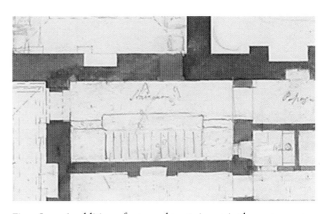

Fig.5. Soane's addition of a secondary staircase in the passageway (SM 34/1/16)

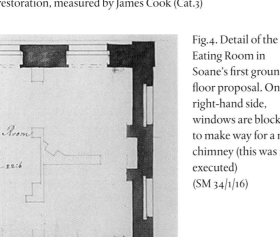

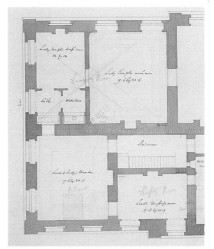

Fig.4. Detail of the Eating Room in Soane's first ground floor proposal. On the right-hand side, windows are blocked to make way for a new chimney (this was not executed) (SM 34/1/16)

Fig.6. Annotations on Soane's plan in the hand of Buckingham, creating a third large room on the ground floor in place of Lady Temple's apartments (Cat.6)

Fig.7. Soane's first proposal for the new Hall. This became Buckingham's favourite design (Cat.9)

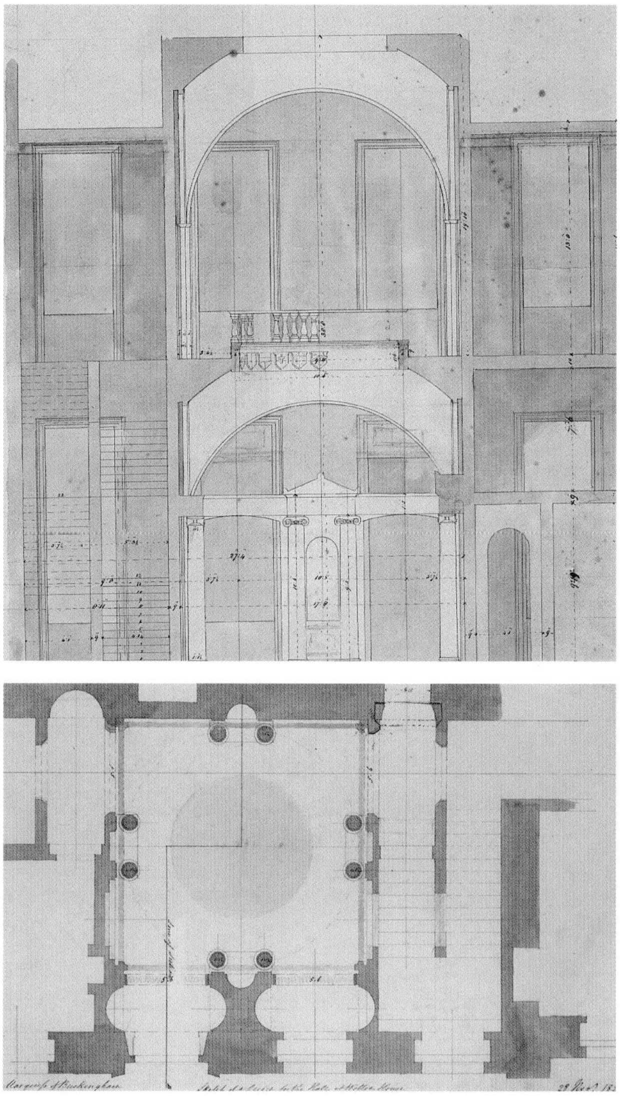

There was one drawing Soane must have wished he had left at home, and that was the perspective of a curious barrel-vaulted Hall (Fig.7). After the meeting the architect quickly rejected this drawing but the design struck a chord with his client who set his mind on having it. In later letters Buckingham calls it 'perfect'[8] and 'better calculated to accord with the space they have to devote to it and to keep the house warm'.[9] Although sensitive to matters of comfort Soane must have been frustrated that his more ambitious plans for the Hall were not exciting his client. Lord Grenville was no more supportive of Soane. After initially approving Soane's tribune designs,[10] he then joined his father in praising the early design, adding a suggestion to extend the barrel-vault over the staircase 'to give a greater appearance of size, as well as throwing in more light'.[11] Soane's tactic seems to have been to ignore these comments and press on with the work, leaving a final decision until March 1821.

Having dropped the barrel-vault hall Soane turned to a favourite solution, a double-height top-lit space, or tribune, based on earlier designs for Lincoln's Inn Fields, Tyringham and the National Debt Redemption Office.[12] As early as 28 November 1820 Soane was immersed in the process of working out how his new tribune could be inserted within the rectangular Hall. His first solution was to introduce lozenge-shaped vestibules on the entrance side, covering the Hall itself with a dome pierced by a circular balustraded opening – an arrangement he repeated on the upper storey (Fig.8). This configuration became 'Design A', which is

Fig.8. First proposal for a double-height tribune in the Hall, with two vestibules on the entrance side. Section (Cat.12) and plan (Cat.11)

shown in two perspective views made prior to Soane's meeting with Lord Grenville at Dropmore on 8 December 1820 (Fig.9). 'Design B' had an oval plan similar to that at Tyringham (Fig.10), and 'Design D', which became Soane's favourite, shifted the whole arrangement to the eastern end of the room (Fig.11). This last design incorporated a ring of columns at first-floor level inspired by the Pitt Memorial at the National Debt Redemption Office designed by Soane in 1818 (Fig.12).

In January 1821 Soane sent a number of drawings to Buckingham and Grenville during which time the work at Wotton proceeded slowly.[13] In March, when the worst of the winter was over, Soane visited the site where he met Grenville. There are two surviving plans with alterations made by Soane in black ink during his visit on 25 March. As

Fig.9. Two versions of Design A for the tribune (Cats 18 & 19)

well as resolving the position of the two main staircases he also sketches in his latest tribune design (Fig.13). By this time it appears that the early barrel-vault design has been forgotten and it is this new arrangement – a rectangular gallery with circular oculus above – which was built.

At this stage it appears that the question of whether or not to lower the roof had not yet been resolved. In a letter dated 29 March Grenville airs his concerns over Soane's proposed elevation and states his preference for the house to remain ' . . . in status quo, provided you can guarantee its safety as of course all my family would be anxious that

as little alteration as possible should take place in the appearance of the exterior'.[14] Soane, in total command of the situation, then suggests deferring the work. This puts Grenville in a panic and two days later Soane's will prevails. It appears the architect convinces his client that there are safety issues involved. This is revealed in a letter from Grenville to Soane written two days later urging him to press on with the work:

'. . . I perceive that from your letter that the building, were it to remain as *formerly, without being lowered*, would be *less* substantial, by which I conclude you mean *less safe*, I cannot of course feel any dislike at the proceedings being continued for lowering it immediately, which I understood you intended should be commenced this week.'[15]

Whatever the nature of the safety concerns raised by Soane (whether to do with fire risk or structural weakness) one can be sure that they were brought up in order to push through his plan to lower the house, a plan that he had first put on paper just a few days after the fire. By leaving the resolution of the issue until this late point in the work he succeeds in rushing his client into agreement.

Although the roof level had been decided, the design of Soane's new Hall was yet to be finalised and it is this feature that becomes the subject of the penultimate group of Wotton drawings. It is only when these drawings are scrutinised that the brilliance of Soane's solution can be fully understood. Soane's earlier designs grappled, unsuccessfully, with the problem of inserting a light-well on a square plan within the rectangular hall (the oval hall of 'Design D' was rejected early on). Soane's final design employs a rectangular first-floor gallery with curved ends

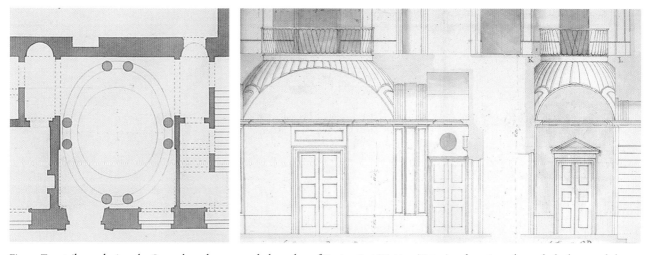

Fig.10. Two tribune designs by Soane based on an oval plan: plan of Design B at Wotton (Cat.13) and sections through the long and short sides of the tribune at Tyringham (SM 3/5/37)

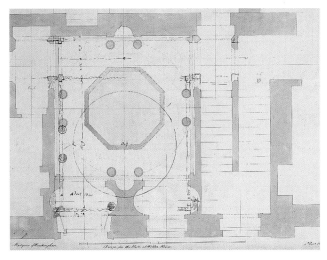

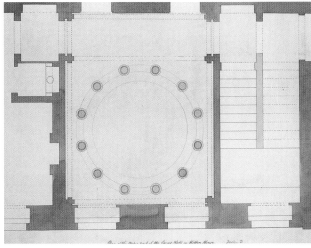

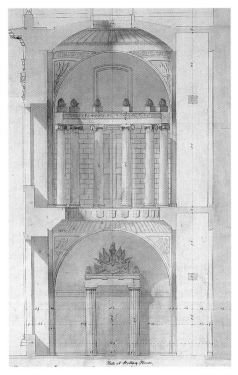

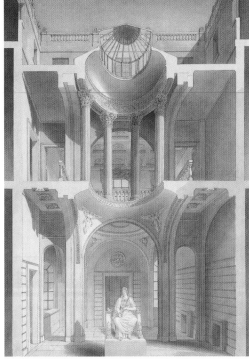

Fig.11. Plans of ground and first floor of the proposed tribune, with the opening shifted to the entrance side (Cats 14 & 16)

Fig.12. The ring of columns at the first floor of Wotton's tribune derived from Soane's design for the Pitt Memorial at the National Debt Redemption Office (Cat.20 and SM 14/4/13)

Fig.13. The final design for the tribune: a rectangular opening surmounted by a circular oculus (Cat.23)

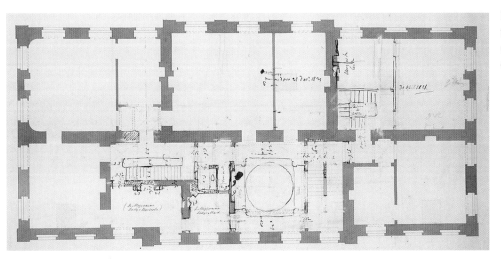

Fig.14. Hanging canopies in the Library at No.13 Lincoln's Inn Fields and at Wotton as drawn by Ptolemy Dean (detail of Cat.49)

Photo: Martin Charles

and, above, a circular opening leads into a strange internal dome in the attic storey carrying a small glazed lantern. The staircase wall is dissolved by an arched opening in the centre at ground floor level and three arched openings on the floor above. In the attic storey semi-circular lunettes allow light in from the east window.

Beneath the gallery the complicated arrangements of columns and shallow dome proposed in earlier drawings is replaced by a hanging canopy reminiscent of that in the Library at 13 Lincoln's Inn Fields (Fig.14), but with panels designed to take heraldic emblems.[16] The gallery above, perhaps as a concession to the client, has an ironwork balustrade based on that in the old house (and possibly reusing certain sections). The opening into the attic storey is ringed with acroteria as in the Pitt Memorial (Fig.15). The result must have been magnificent – light would have

Fig.15. Soane arranged a ring of acroteria around the top of the upper oculus at Wotton (Cat.27). This recalled his designs for the Pitt Memorial at the National Debt Redemption Office (SM P401)

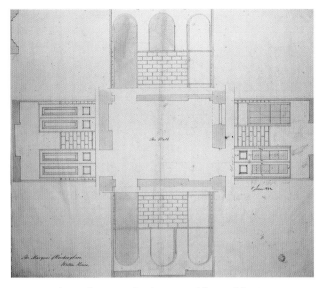

Fig.16. Laid-out elevations for the ground floor of the Entrance Hall, showing the rustication to dado level (Cat.28)

Fig.17. Reconstruction of the tribune as built, drawn by Ptolemy Dean (Cat.49) © Ptolemy Dean, 2004

streamed in from the windows and doorway on the ground and first floors, and the dome above would have been glowed with the gentle diffused light admitted through the small lantern and front window. Like the entrance hall at No.13 Lincoln's Inn Fields, the ground floor is rusticated to dado level (Fig.16) with the other surfaces grained to varying shades.[17]

The tribune at Wotton, so sadly lost to alterations in the 1920s, is restored in Ptolemy Dean's watercolour, commissioned by *Country Life* (Fig.17).

The lost tribune may have been the most important architectural feature of Soane's redesign but it was the north-south spine corridor that represented the most significant planning innovation of the new house. This corridor, envisaged by Soane from the earliest design stages, linked all three staircases, freeing up the circulation of house, and allowing apartments on the north side to be accessed by a side door. Initially Soane intended the northern end of the passageway to be composed of a series of lobbies (Fig.18) but this was simplified in the final design to a sequence of arched openings. This ingenious perspective device was a favourite Soane feature, appearing at Dulwich Picture Gallery, Aynhoe Park, and the loggia in the Governor's Court at the Bank of England (1803) (Fig.19). In the southern section of the passageway the spatial experience is very different. After passing across the tribune, the passageway rises to take in the mezzanine level above (another of Soane's additions for the sake of comfort); a door with railed aperture above then opens out into the secondary stair.

The finishing of the rooms is recorded in a final group of drawings. The simplicity of the detailing reflects the economic and time pressures under which Soane was working.[18] There are no vaulted or domed ceilings (although that of the Saloon is coved as a homage to the earlier

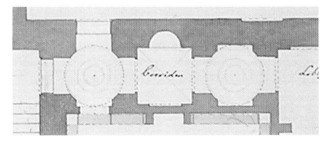

Fig.18. A sequence of lobbies in an early design of the south end of the new passageway (Cat.6)

Fig.19. Arched openings in the loggia of the Governor's Court at the Bank of England and as completed in the corridor at Wotton House
Left photo: F R Yerbury
Right photo: Country Life Picture Library

house[19]) and Soane's detailing is restrained, confined predominantly to reed and ball mouldings. The Drawing Room is given curved corners, a feature which was later to delight Elaine Brunner when revealed beneath 1920s panelling.

By the end of 1822 the house was nearing completion, and Buckingham seemed delighted with the progress. In a letter to Soane dated 2 October 1822 he '... rejoiced to find that the rebuilding of Wotton has gone on so professionally. That it does you credit, is no more than I was sure it would. In fact I hear that it is a *beautiful* piece of work'.[20]

The house was finally ready for habitation in early 1823 although there were a number of teething problems. Buckingham wrote to Soane in February 1823 calling his attention to 'some extraordinary instances of neglect on the part of the Clerk of Works, in consequence of which the house has already had a very narrow escape from being again burned down' and complaining about the chimneys '... all of which smoke to a degree which renders the house uninhabitable.'[21] These problems continued into 1824 – the roof leaked and there were the usual signs of settlement with cracks appearing on the

back staircase and in some ceilings.[22] James Cook visited the house in May 1824 and his report is sanguine: '... the work stands much better than I could have expected, considering the short time allowed to compleat the business ... When the Marquis of Chandos finishes painting the house it will require a good joiner to rehang the shutters, sashes etc, and a good plasterer to wash and stop the walls and ceilings ... as all buildings are obliged to be done after a certain time when the work is got settled to its proper bearings.'[23] Soane finally submitted his bill in March 1826.[24]

What Soane achieved at Wotton was remarkable both for its simplicity and grandeur. The reorganisation of the interior showed an intuitive appreciation of the demands of modern living (such as the need for privacy and comfort), the north-south passageway established one of Soane's most exciting internal vistas and the Tribune, with its blending of geometric forms and its delicate hanging canopy heralded the exceptional spatial complexity and curiously Gothic spirit of Soane's work at the Law Courts (Fig.20). Its reinstatement would give us back one of Soane's most spectacular domestic spaces.

Fig.20. Interior of the Court of the Chancery, drawn by Joseph Michael Gandy, c.1825 (SM 16/1/2)

1   Ptolemy Dean, *Sir John Soane and the Country Estate*, London, 1999.

2   The extensive body of Wotton material in the Soane archive includes correspondence, progress reports from the Clerk of Works and tradesman's bills. This material has recently been catalogued and a copy is available for study in the Research Library at the Soane Museum.

3   Here, Lord Buckingham is used for Richard Temple-Nugent-Brydges-Chandos Grenville, 2nd Marquess of Buckingham (1776–1839) who was created Duke of Buckingham and Chandos in 1822, and Lord Grenville is used for his son Richard Plantagenet later 2nd Duke (1797–1861), referred to in the SM correspondence as Earl Temple from Jan. 1821.

4   Buckingham House in Pall Mall was built between 1792 and 1795, see p.23.

5   Soane had carried out a number of alterations at Stowe, see pp.24–26.

6   Journal 6, 17 Nov 1820.

7   Comparison with correspondence reveals that the pencil notes on drawings 34/1/15 & 34/1/17 are in Buckingham's hand.

8   Priv. Corr. XIII.C.3.12. 26 Dec. 1820.

9   Priv. Corr. XIII.C.3.16. 19 Jan. 1821.

10 Priv. Corr. XIII.C.3.8. 17 Dec. 1821.

11 Priv. Corr. XIII.C.3.17. 8 Feb. 1821.

12 The Dome Area at Lincoln's Inn Fields was constructed in 1812–13; the Entrance Vestibule at Tyringham in 1795–7 and the Pitt Memorial at the National Debt Redemption Office in 1817–18.

13 Journal 6: 6 Jan.; 11 Jan.; 27 Jan. 1821.

14 Priv. Corr. XIII.C.3.25.1. 29 Mar. 1821.

15 Priv. Corr. XIII.C.3.25.1. 31 Mar. 1821.

16 The Grenvilles had a deep interest in their dynastic roots. Soane's Gothic library at Stowe (see p.24) was rich in heraldic decoration.

17 Soane's pencil notes on the tribune section drawing 34/1/30 record the graining scheme.

18 For a more detailed account of Buckingham's financial problems see p.26.

19 Lord Temple writes to Soane on 19 Sept 1822 (Priv. Corr. XIII. C.3.80): 'Respecting the ceilings of the three large rooms, I should prefer them coved, being in my opinion handsomer.'

20 Priv. Corr. XIII.C.3.73.

21 Priv. Corr. XIII.C.3.77. 9 Feb. 1823.

22 8/88/106. Letter from Buckingham to Soane. 1 May 1824.

23 8/88/4.

24 Ledger E., p.149. Soane calculated the total cost of works at £12,767 and his own fee (5% plus expenses) at £807.18.0. He re-submitted his bill five times over the next six years, on the final occasion to Mr Robson, a solicitor who was now dealing with the Duke's affairs. There is no evidence that Soane was ever paid for his work.

CATALOGUE

This exhibition features a careful selection of the fifty or so drawings and two hundred documents in Soane's collection that relate to the Wotton project. A majority of the drawings were made in Soane's office at Lincoln's Inn Fields between November 1820 and January 1821 and the work was shared between George Bailey, Edward Foxhall, Charles Papendiek and Arthur Mee. Although the drawings are unsigned (other than Cat.1) an examination of the office Day Books reveals that Mee worked almost exclusively on perspective views whilst Foxhall drew most of the plans.

All catalogue entries by William Palin other than 33–48 & 50 by William Palin and Isabelle Flour.

Cat.5

A NOTE ON ABBREVIATIONS

PD = Ptolemy Dean, *Sir John Soane and the Country Estate*, London, 1999
Country Life, July 1949 = Gordon Nares, 'Wotton House, Buckinghamshire I-III', *Country Life*, 1, 7, 15 July 1949
Country Life, 13 May 2004 = Giles Worsley, 'Wotton House', *Country Life*, 13 May 2004
Apollo, April 2004 = Peter Inskip, 'Soane and the Grenvilles', *Apollo*, April 2004

1 Reconstruction drawing from survey sketches showing pre-fire entrance front. Signed by James Cook, the Clerk of Works

Insc: *Elevation of the Entrance Front of Wotton House previous to its restoration after the Fire in 1820/ Made by Jas. Cook/* [in another hand] *To Dig Brick Earth at Wotton to Make Bricks*
Pencil, pen and wash (502 x 687)
34/1/3

On receiving news of the fire at Wotton Soane immediately dispatched his trusted assistant James Cook to inspect the damage. Cook arrived at Wotton on 31 October and found the roof, floors and bond timbers all completely destroyed, and many of the partition walls severely damaged. He then began the difficult task of surveying the house, clambering through the smouldering ruins and taking measurements from the surviving fabric. His first letter to Soane (Cat.33) is stoical, '. . . according to your wish' he writes 'I am getting all the dimensions I can'. Soane himself arrived at the house the following day.

This drawing, presumably made from sketches taken on site, would have provided the information for the 'split' elevation which Soane presented to Buckingham in London a week after the fire (Cat.4).

2 Longitudinal section of house after the fire

Insc: *Section of Wotton House – after the fire in 1820*
Pencil and pen with grey and yellow washes (497 x 675)
34/1/44

The forlorn shell of the great house is dramatically illustrated in this section taken through the garden front. It shows the surviving masonry walls, doorway openings and chimney flues. The large cracks above many of the openings reflect the precarious state of the ruin. Soane would have worked from this drawing when realigning the floor levels in his new design. (see p.28)

3 Survey plan of basement and principal floors prior to Soane's alterations

Insc: *Plans of Wotton House previous to its renovation in 1821 after the Fire in 1820*
Pencil, pen and grey wash (528 x 732)
34/1/5
Lit: *Country Life*, May 2004, p.110

In spite of the devastation, Soane's Clerk of Works at Wotton, James Cook, was still able to decipher the pre-fire plan forms of the ground

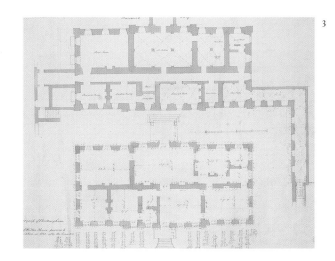

storey and basement from surviving masonry walls. Although Soane was to make very few changes to the basement plan, he made a series of important alterations to the ground storey (see Cat.6). The basement plan shows groin vaulted ceilings that survived the fire (these were retained by Soane) and the sunken passage to the north pavilion, with its *oeil-de-boeuf* windows.

4 Presentation drawing showing part elevations of the pre-fire entrance front and the proposed design for its restoration

Insc: [beneath left half of elevation] *as it existed previous to the fire . . .* [beneath right half] *as designed to be restored 1820/ Entrance Front of Wotton House Bucks*
Pencil, pen and wash (335 x 460)
34/1/1
Lit: PD p. 152; *Apollo* April 2004 p.21

Produced in Soane's office with the help of James Cook's survey sketches, this small drawing was almost certainly the 'Elevation, as proposed' that Soane showed to Lord Buckingham at Buckingham House, Pall Mall on 7 November 1820. The Day Books record that Bailey and Foxhall were 'About plans of Wotton House' on that day. It shows the pre-fire elevation beside Soane's proposed lowered design.

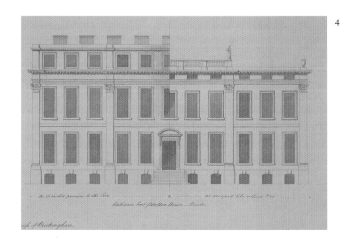

5 *Presentation drawing showing elevation of entrance front as proposed with outline of original chimneystacks indicated by dotted line*

Insc: *Design for the entrance front of Wotton House, Bucks*
Dated: *Lincoln's Inn Fields Nov. 1820*
Pencil, pen and watercolour with ruled and washed border (645 x 961)
34/1/2

On 17 November 1820 Soane travelled to Stowe to continue discussions with Buckingham. He took with him four plans; perspective views of the Hall and Library, and one large elevation. This drawing is almost certainly the elevation in question, or a copy made for the office and reveals how little the built elevation differed from his earliest designs.

In this design the original basement and ground floor configuration of the house are retained whilst the upper two storeys are lowered, with the attic storey inserted behind the entablature. The attic windows are reduced to a single pane in height and placed in the frieze. The central 5-bay section, framed by giant Corinthian pilasters, is given added emphasis with the inclusion of a stone balustrade (a Palladian motif) surmounted by a statue at each end. The balustrade was omitted in the final design. The pilasters at each end of the façade are topped by urns, as in the original house.

By lowering the entire elevation Soane turns an overtly late-Baroque house into a more 'proper' classical composition, emphasising broadness rather than height. Soane's one dramatic departure from the classical model is his decision to retain the nine prominent chimneystacks which, although lowered in his design, were not reduced until the restoration work of the 1950s and 60s. (see p.37)

6 *Plan of the proposed ground floor with pencil annotations by Buckingham. Design C No.1*

Insc: *Design for the principal floor of Wotton House./ The Marquis of Buckingham* [In pencil] *Design C. No.1./ As altered and finally agreed at Stowe*
Dated: *Lincoln's Inn Fields/ Nov. 1820*
Pencil, pen and watercolour (647 x 965)
34/1/15

A good deal of business was conducted during Soane's visit to Stowe on 17 November 1820. This drawing, one of four plans taken by Soane on that occasion, has been annotated by Buckingham himself (the hand matches that of his letters). Buckingham's changes (made in

pencil) generally relate to the allotted functions for the rooms. Thus, he moves Lord and Lady Temple's apartments to another floor, and replaces them with a bedroom, dressing room and large garden-facing drawing room. Soane's grand library (shown in perspective Cat.10) is rejected – Buckingham replaces this with a 'Bed Room'. The other important change is the addition of a side entrance giving access to the north-south corridor.

7 *Plan of the proposed first floor with pencil annotations by Buckingham. Design C No.1*

Insc: *The Plan of the Chamber Floor of Wotton House. Design C No 1/ The Marquis of Buckingham*
Dated: *Lincoln's Inn Fields/ Nov. 1820*
Pencil, pen and watercolour (638 x 952)
34/1/17

Like Cat.6 this plan has been amended by Buckingham. He has relocated the private apartments of Lord and Lady Temple to this floor (where they form a suite of rooms on the south side of the house). He has also changed the small chamber and larger billiard room (with a starfish-vaulted ceiling) to a library (originally sited on the first floor) and bedroom. The 'upper part of the Hall' is now a square within the rectangular vestibule.

8 *Designs for the proposed Hall and Library. Sections and plan of Hall on left side in Soane's hand. Plan of Library and passageway and unidentified pencil sketch on right*

Insc: *Sketch of a Design for The Hall. Wotton House*
Dated: *L.I.F. Sunday 12 Nov. 1820*
Pencil, pen and watercolour (576 x 694)
34/1/29

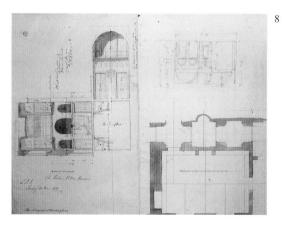

8

During the week following his first post-fire meeting with Buckingham, Soane worked on solutions for the Hall. The sketches on the left of the sheet relate to the barrel vault design shown in perspective in Cat.9 ('Design C'). This was to become a favourite of Buckingham's and as late as February 1821 he was urging Soane to adopt it.

The coloured section shows the south side of the room as a double-height space with two slightly curved galleries running north-south at either end of the room. In the centre the barrel-vaulted ceiling forms a semi-circle in profile, rising from first floor dado level. Consol brackets have been drawn under the gallery.

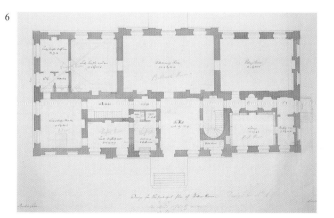

6

9 Perspective view of Hall as proposed. Design C

Insc: *Design C/ View of the Great Hall in Wotton House*
Signed and dated: *John Soane Archt/ Nov: 1820*
Pencil, pen and watercolour (456 × 272)
34/1/36
Lit: *Country Life* July 1949 p. 183; PD p.153 *Apollo* April 2004 p. 22

Soane's first solution for the new Hall was unlike any of the designs that would follow. This drawing was one of those taken by Soane to Stowe on 17 November 1820 (the Journal mentions a 'perspective of the hall') and was developed from the sketched design (Cat.8). In this view (looking west) the main architectural components of the hall are visible. The hall is broken into three parts: a barrel vaulted and coffered ceiling over the central part of the room, and two flanking double-height spaces. On the west side at first floor level is a slim curving gallery with a balustrade supported by console brackets – this links doors on the north, south and west. It appears that an identical balustrade was intended for the east side, although it is omitted from this view so as not to obscure the other elements of the design. The ceiling in the foreground, above the east gallery is also coffered.

The ground floor is rusticated up to door height with inset panels and roundels on the north and south sides. Also on the north and south sides, above door height, are three arched openings with balustrades (those on the south appear to be blank). This feature finds its way, in an altered form, into Soane's final designs. A row of shields appears under the west gallery – as at Stowe Buckingham was keen that heraldic display should feature in the architecture of his new house (Cats 47 & 48). (see p.30)

10 Perspective view of proposed Library

Insc: *Wotton house/ View of Library*
Dated: *L.I.Fields/ 15 Nov: 1820*
Pencil, pen and watercolour (231 × 235)
34/1/37
Lit: *Country Life* July 1949 p. 183

On Soane's early plans the Library was located on the ground floor. At this stage Soane was still exploring how the floor levels might be altered to accommodate new double-height spaces.

In this perspective view of the envisaged Library the ground storey is lined by bookcases and the upper level is given an Ionic colonnade. On two sides of the room the columns are set in the round in front of walls lined by statuary and on the far side is a gallery where the columns are paired and the plinths linked by an iron balustrade. Behind this is a three-part bookcase. This view was presented to Buckingham during Soane's visit to Stowe in November 1820, and was dropped shortly afterwards, perhaps as a result the client's decision to move the Library to the first floor.

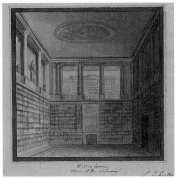

10

11 Plan for proposed Hall at ground floor level overlaid with 'Line of Section'

Insc: *Sketch of a Design for the Hall at Wotton House*
Dated: *28 Nov. 1820*
Pencil and pen with grey and pink washes (344 × 559)
34/1/25

One of Soane's solutions for the Hall at Wotton involved the introduction of two small lozenge-shaped vestibules in front of the eastern door and window. This gave him a square plan in which to design his new tribune. On this design he places paired columns on each side and draws in a circular oculus above. This drawing is one of a series under the heading 'Design A'. It was presented to Lord Grenville at Dropmore on 8–9 December 1820 together with other drawings (see also Cats 12, 18 & 19). (see p.30)

12 North-south section through proposed Entrance Hall looking east. Design A.

Insc: *Hall, Wotton House/* [In pencil] *Design A*
Dated: *29 November 1820*
Pencil, pen and watercolour (742 × 534)
34/1/45

By the time of the Wotton project, the double-height hall, or tribune, had become one of Soane's favourite architectural features. He had already employed this feature for the entrance vestibule at Tyringham, Buckinghamshire (*c.*1800), the Dome Area at his Museum (1812–13) and at the National Debt Redemption Office (1817–18).

This section for the Wotton tribune is the earliest surviving drawing for what was to become the most important and controversial part of the whole building project. It was produced by Soane following his meeting with Buckingham at Stowe on 17 November 1820 and is based on 'Design A' (see Cat.11). It shows a double-height space with the upper dome rising into the attic storey of the house. The view east shows the two small vestibules in front of the door and window between which is a niche flanked by Ionic columns carrying an entablature and Grecian pediment. The heraldic shields (which appear in nearly all the tribune designs) and balustrade around the ring of the oculus are also drawn in.

One small but telling pencil alteration to the section, probably by Soane himself, is the raising of the door height to match the window (a typical example of the architect's acute sensitivity to symmetry and balance). On the right of the drawing the mezzanine level is visible (which was built as drawn). This was inserted above the closet and chamber to the east of the secondary staircase to provide additional servants' quarters and is also shown in plan on Cats 23 & 25.

13 Plan of the ground floor as proposed. Design B

Insc: *The Plan of the Ground Floor of Wotton House. Design B*
Dated: *December 1820*
Pencil, pen and grey wash (620 × 955)
34/1/14

Here in 'Design B' Soane presents his clients with another option for the treatment of the new Hall. Soane eliminates the eastern vestibules of 'Design A' and creates an oval dome supported by paired columns, rising to a circular oculus. The grand staircase is reversed with the upward flight moved to the north side, leaving an entrance space with

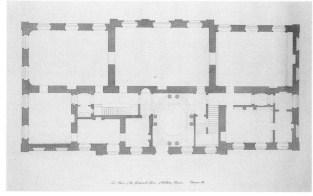

13

apsidal ends to the north-west of the Hall (matched by an identical space on the opposite side). Like 'Design A', this scheme was destined to be rejected.

14 *Plan for the Hall at ground floor level overlaid with new design in pen in Soane's hand*

Insc: *Design for the Hall at Wotton House*
Dated: *4th Dec. 1820*
Pencil and pen with grey and pink washes (520 x 730)
34/1/24

The surviving drawings for the Hall at Wotton show Soane grappling with the problem of how to position his new tribune within the rectangular space. Here Soane himself has sketched a new design over an existing drawing. Unhappy with the 'Design A' configuration in which the tribune is placed positioned to the west, he pushes the whole arrangement to the east, eliminating the lozenge vestibules (which Soane may have felt interfered with the natural lighting of the room). He makes his changes in pen, drawing the circular opening in the ceiling above (replacing an octagonal gallery) and moving the columns on the south side on axis with the centre of the opening.

This new configuration brings its own architectural disharmonies however. Soane is left with two stranded columns on the west side, breaking the symmetry of the plan, and he seems to realise this as he half-heartedly sketches in just one column on the east side. (see p.32)

15 *Plan of the Hall. Design D*

Insc: *Plan of the Great Hall in Wotton House.* [In pencil] *Design D*
Dated: *Dec. 1820*
Pencil, pen and grey wash (620 x 937)
34/1/21

15

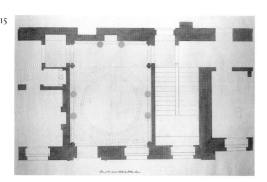

Here, the eastern side of the Hall is surmounted by a shallow dome which rises to a large oculus. The scallop decoration on the underside of the canopy recalls the treatment of other Soane domes such as the drawing-room ceiling at Wimpole Hall. There are paired columns on the north, south and west sides of the room, those at the west flanking a fireplace.

The principal stair is shown with a landing rather than a curved sweep which identifies it with Soane's early designs.

16 *Plan for the Hall at first floor level. Design D*

Insc: *Plan of the Upper Part of the Great Hall in Wotton House.*
[In pencil] *Design D*
Dated: *December 1820*
Pencil, pen and grey wash (626 x 936)
34/1/22

This is the plan belongs with 34/1/21 and shows how Soane imagined the 'Great Hall' developing on the next level. A ring of 12 columns surrounds the circular opening and support another level above. This design borrows elements from the Pitt Cenotaph at the National Debt Redemption Office. (see p.32)

17 *Perspective view of the Hall as proposed. Design B*

Insc: *Design B/ View of the Great Hall in Wotton House*
Signed and dated: *John Soane Archt/ Decr 1820*
Pencil, pen and watercolour (506 x 286)
34/1/35
Lit: PD p.153

On 8–9 December 1820 Soane visited Lord Grenville at Dropmore. He took with him a series of designs including this watercolour (Cats 18 & 19 also belong to this group). It shows the view west through the proposed Hall. The wall surfaces on the ground floor are given a plain treatment and there are arched blank openings either side of the paired columns on the west side. The dome above is circular and is positioned to the east end of the hall, with the corridor running across the far end. The other elements are treated as in Cat.18, although here a lantern has been sketched in pencil above the upper oculus.

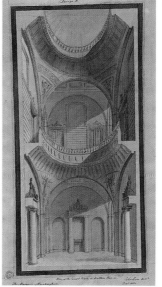

17

18 Perspective view of the Hall as proposed. Design A.1

Insc: *Design A.1./ View of the Great Hall in Wotton House*
Signed and dated: *John Soane Archt/ Decr 1820*
Pencil, pen and watercolour (491 x 265)
34/1/33

This view relates to the section Cat.12. Here, Soane positions the tribune at the western end of the entrance vestibule. The architectural detailing and decoration of the ground floor is more elaborate than in Cat.17. Soane employs paired fluted Ionic columns with thin bases to frame niches and statuary, and the walls are given horizontal rustication. As in Cat.12, the dome above has a circular oculus with stone balustrade. The underside of the dome is enriched with a scallop decoration and winged angels in the spandrels (both familiar Soanean details).

The gallery storey has doors on the north and south sides and a 'landing' above the ground floor corridor. Above this level is another dome with an oculus and balustrade above. (see p.31)

19 Perspective view of the Hall as proposed. Design A.2

Insc: *Design A.2./ View of the Great Hall in Wotton House*
Signed and dated: *John Soane Archt/ Decr 1820*
Pencil, pen and watercolour (465 x 256)
34/1/34

Like Cat.18 this perspective relates to the section Cat.12. It shows the view east and is modelled on 'Design A', although the two vestibules are absent. (see p.31)

20 Section of Hall as proposed looking south

Insc: *Hall at Wotton House*
Dated: *L.I.F./ Dec. 12. 1820*
Pencil, pen and watercolour (731 x 514)
34/1/26
Lit: PD p. 150; *Apollo* April 2004 p.23

This ring of 12 Ionic columns around the first floor gallery recalls Soane's memorial for William Pitt at the National Debt Redemption Office (1817–18). This design is one of a group of three sections (see Cats 21 & 22).

Paired baseless Doric columns on the ground floor support trophies and helmets, and a dome above springs seamlessly from four corner piers. The ring of unfluted Ionic columns above carries a continuous decorated entablature on which are placed helmets (possibly intended to be bronze). (see p.32)

21 Section of Hall looking west. Design D

Insc: *Section of the Hall at Wotton House/ Design D*
Dated: *13th Dec. 1820*
Pencil, pen and watercolour (728 x 512)
34/1/27

This is the same design as Cat.20, this time showing the view west. On the west wall the paired Doric columns flank a fireplace.

22 Section of the Hall looking west. Design D. No.2

Insc: *Section of the Great Hall in Wotton House. /Design D. No 2*
Dated: *Dec. 1820* [under south side] *11 Dec. 1820*
Pencil, pen and watercolour (912 x 620)
34/1/28

In this variant of Cats 20 & 21 an unfluted Ionic order is used for the ground floor and an iron strigulated balustrade is placed between the columns above. A stone balustrade also appears above the oculus on the second floor.

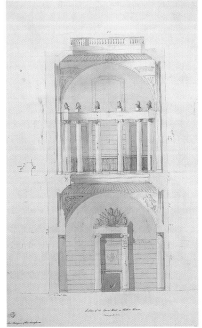

23 Plan of first floor with amendments in Soane's hand. Design A

Insc: *The Plan of the Chamber Floor of Wotton House. Design A*
Dated: *December, 1820*
Pencil, pen and grey wash (625 x 948)
34/1/13

Soane stayed at Wotton on 23 to 25 March and 28 April to 1 May 1821 and the amendments to this plan (helpfully dated), were made by Soane on site.

Soane's alterations include the moving of a partition in the north-west chamber (which has been rubbed out and moved to align with that in the north-east room), and the addition of a staircase around a square stairwell at the east end of the room (inscribed 'stairway to attic'). In the room to the west of the staircase Soane has moved the chimney 'to the centre' (Soane was always a stickler for symmetry).

The most significant changes relate to the tribune and secondary staircase. Soane moves the circular oculus in the tribune to the east so it occupies the centre of the landing space. He narrows the doorways to the flanking rooms and, most importantly, rubs out most of the staircase partition, opening it out into the 'Gallery' and the hall. (see p.32)

24 Plan of the Ground or Principal Floor

Insc: *Plan of the Principal Floor of Wotton House as restored, 1821*
Pencil, pen and grey wash (506 x 717)
34/1/7
Lit: PD p. 152; *Country Life*, May 2004, p.110

This plan is one of a set showing the plan of the house as built (see also Cats 25 & 26). Soane has created an Eating Room in the north-west corner from what were, in the old house, three smaller rooms. This new space balances the Drawing Room in the south-west and completes the sequence of grand rooms on the garden front of the house. Soane has also moved the interconnecting doorways to the centre of each wall creating a clear north-south axis (marked on the plan together with the east-west axis). A more subtle change is the addition of curved corners at the south end of the Drawing Room.

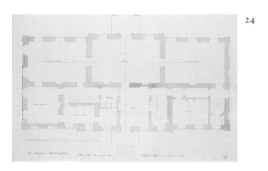

24

On the east side Soane has extended the existing corridor into the Bed Chamber creating a new north-south axis running the full length of the house. A new entrance on the north side leads straight into this corridor. Soane added three new staircases, one (at the north end) serving the basement only, one (to the south) rising the full height of the house around a rectangular well and, of course a new central staircase rising up from the ground to the first floor behind a pierced wall giving views into the new Hall (the architectural features of which were unresolved at the time this plan was made).

The asymmetrical placing of the new Hall is something which still puzzles visitors to Wotton. The main reason for this seems to be that the wall on the left of the entrance hall is a load-bearing partition and carries a chimney flue from the basement – its retention was thus a cost-saving measure. What is clear also from Soane's subsequent designs for the Hall is that the restrictions of this space, imposed by the original house plan, lent itself to the vertiginous drama of his double-height entrance vestibule.

25 Plan of the first floor as restored

Insc: *Plan of the Chamber Floor of Wotton House as restored, 1821*
Pencil, pen and grey wash (506 x 720)
34/1/8

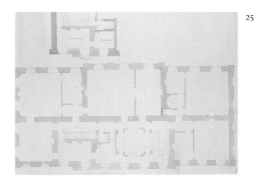

25

Comfort and privacy were two important considerations in the designing of the new Wotton. One of Soane's innovations was the addition of a mezzanine level at the south-east corner for the lady's maid, reached via the secondary staircase. This half-floor drops down behind the upper panes of the tall windows on the left of the entrance front.

Soane introduced another staircase behind a partition on the south side of the north-west corner chamber leading to the servants' quarters in the attic. These new staircases were added for flexibility and comfort and enabled the house to be divided between family and guest apartments (a feature which makes Wotton, a very large house, convenient and manageable as a family dwelling even today). Other domestic improvements include the blocking off of certain windows in corner rooms to give them warmth and privacy.

26 Plan of the attic floor as restored

Insc: *Plan of the attic Story of Wotton House, as restored, 1821*
Pencil, pen and grey wash (506 x 718)
34/1/9

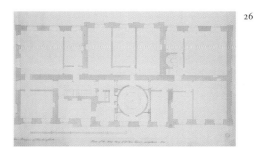

26

The dominating feature of the attic storey plan is the upper level of the tribune with its domed ceiling marked in. At this level the tribune was not directly accessible but could be admired from openings on the west and east side of the dome.

27 Sections through the Hall, looking east (left side) and north. Overlaid with pencil notes relating to the decorative scheme in Soane's hand

Insc: *Section of the Hall at Wotton House, 1821*
Pencil, pen and grey wash (586 x 528)
34/1/30
Lit: PD p. 154

These sections represent Soane's final design for the Hall – the last unresolved element of the new Wotton House. Soane's solution to the problem of how to position and light his new tribune is original and brilliant and shown in perspective in Ptolemy Dean's watercolour (Cat.49).

27

The first important deviation from the earlier designs (Cats 9 & 17–19), is the reshaping of the ground storey and the gallery above. The ground floor level is now open, occupying the entire Hall and so taking in the north-south corridor. The opening above forms a rectangular gallery with curved corners. A wooden canopy, inset with panels carrying shields, hangs from the gallery and is linked to walls by arched panels (reminiscent of his canopies in the Library at 13 Lincoln's Inn Fields and a number of his ceilings for the Law Courts). On the ground floor the paired columns of earlier designs are absent and Soane instead concentrates on introducing spatial freedom by dissolving portions of the staircase wall. In the centre of the ground floor wall he introduces a half-height round-headed opening and, on the floor above, three more arched apertures open on to the staircase.

On the next level Soane re-uses the iron balustrade from the staircase of the older house around the gallery. The disposition of the windows on the east side is unclear but on the north side (the staircase wall) a wide central section of wall is dissolved and flanked by openings centred on those below. A dome rises to a circular oculus ringed by enclosed palmettes similar to those used on the upper level of the Pitt Memorial at the National Debt Redemption Office. The attic level contains a large secondary dome pierced by an oculus and a small skylight. A curious feature is the introduction of small semi-circular openings on the each side of the base of the

dome. This opening on the east side was presumably intended to allow light to enter from the attic window, and the others were added to give symmetry to the arrangement.

Pencil notes on the left side of the eastern elevation refer to the different bands of decoration on the walls and dome. One can presume that the notes refer to the colour of the grained walls. Much later, in a letter dated 28 July 1826, the Marquis of Chandos hesitates between painting the rustic part of the Hall oak or leaving it stone colour, leaving the decision to Soane. On this section the ground floor is marked 'dark' with an upper band 'lighter'. The first floor has been inscribed 'much lighter' and the dome 'not grained'.

28 Plan and laid-out elevation of the Hall with full size detail of skirting and dado joinery mouldings in profile. Some measurements overlaid in pen and pencil in Soane's hand

Insc: *The Hall/ Wotton House*
Pencil, pen and watercolour (534 x 665)
34/1/40

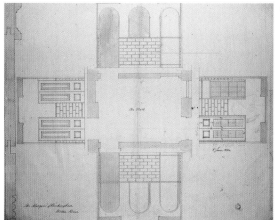

28

This is one of a group of drawings showing the architectural treatment proposed for the principal rooms of the house.

The amendments (in Soane's hand) are to the detailing of the front door and are dated 5 June 1822. On this drawing it is possible to see how the south elevation matches that staircase partition on the north (although the central arched element is blank). On the east side the window and glazed door reflect the two doors (one of which is blank) on the west. The walls are rusticated to dado level and plain above.

29 Sketch profile of great cornice in Soane's hand

Insc: *Great Cornice 1/2 size. Sunday 21st July 1822*
Pencil and pen (528 x 655)
34/1/42 verso

The cornice was one of the last elements of the design to be resolved. This sketch was made by Soane when he was at Wotton House on 21 and 22 July 1822. Here Soane introduces an original and striking feature – a hanging 'acorn'-shaped element placed between the dentils.

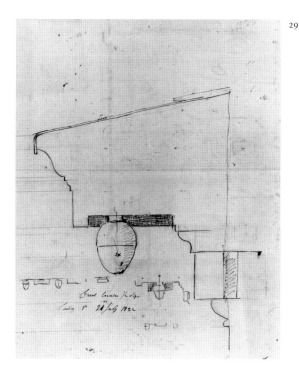

30 Full size details of window joinery with sections and elevations in James Cook's hand

Insc: *Deal cased sash frames/ Oak sunk Cill/ 2 1/2 Inch deal astragal & hollow sashes/ 5/8 Bar*
Dated: *1st August 1821*
Pencil, pen and watercolour (440 x 345)
91/3/5

The sheet is taken up by profiles related to the construction of the sashes and sills. On the right-hand side are elevations and sections relating to windows on the ground and first floors. This indicates that Soane had a standard treatment for all the windows in the house.

31 Design for a chimney-piece with two choices for colour treatment and detailing

Insc: *Veined Slab two feet from the face of pilaster/ Eating Room/ Wotton Hall*
Dated: *20th Octr 1821*
Pencil, pen and watercolour (365 x 509)
81/2/33

Soane presented Grenville with this chimney-piece design in October 1821, and it was approved immediately. It was later copied into a volume of chimney-piece designs and other details – see Cat 32. The black and gold veined marble design (with simple sunk moulding) on the left half of the drawing is similar to the chimney-piece used by Soane in the Breakfast Room at Pitzhanger Manor. The option on the right is white marble with blue veining. It has the same moulding but has an additional two incised Greek fret elements on the rebate. In his letter dated 21 Oct. 1821, Earl Temple ordered it to be made in black and gold. In a letter dated 4 Feb 1822, James Cook informed Soane that the chimney-pieces had all arrived from London and that the dining room one had been put up.

32 Design for a chimney-piece in the Eating Room

Insc: *Veined Slab two feet from the face of the Plaster/ Eating Room/ Wotton Hall*
Dated: *2nd Novr 1821*
Pencil, pen and watercolour (258 x 162)
Vol. 43/18

This was copied into this volume from Cat.31.

33 Letter from Buckingham to John Soane

Priv. Corr. XIII.C.2.17

My dear Sir
I beg to see you immediately without a moments loss of time – Poor Wotton is burnd down –
Yours truly
Chandos Buckingham
Get one of your foremen ready to set off immediately

This letter, penned hastily by a desperate Buckingham just after the devastating fire on the night of 29 October 1820, asks for Soane's immediate assistance. Soane had by this time worked on a number of building projects for Buckingham (see pp.22–7) and this note reflects the strength of trust between the client and his favoured architect.

34 Letter from James Cook to John Soane

Priv. Corr. XIII.C.2.18

Wotton House October 31st 1820

Sir,
According to your Request I took the first Conveyance I could meet with and Arrived at Wootton this morning – the Roof floors and all the Bond timbers are Compleately Destroyed by the fire – and some of the party walls are in a Shattered State – the workmen are Busily employd in clearing away the Rubbish over the groins and Different parts of the Building – there is fire Breaking out in Different parts of the basement at present – According to your wish I am getting all the Dimensions I can against your Arrivall – Earl of Temple is Busily Employed with the work people –
From your Humble Servant
James Cook

Cook arrived at Wotton on 31 October 1820 and shortly afterwards wrote to Soane informing him of the state of the house after the fire. The fact that the ruins were still smouldering must have made life difficult for Cook as he set to work taking measurements from the shell of the building. Cook's measurements formed the data for the survey drawings (Cats 1–3).

35 Letter from Earl Temple to John Soane

Priv. Corr. XIII.C.3.53

Wotton 21 Oct. 1821

I approve highly of the plan for the chimney piece and request you will loose no time in ordering it to be made in black and gold, which is so much better for a dining room.

This relates to the chimney-piece design Cat.31.

36 *Letter from James Cook to John Soane with a drawing showing part elevations of the façade and sections at the level of the chamber floor and the attic storey, before the fire and as restored*

Priv. Corr. XIII.C.3.83

Dated: *Wotton, 8th April 1821*

This letter, with attached drawing, informs Soane of the progress of work. The drawing shows part elevations and sections of the chamber floor and attic storey of the façade. On the left-hand side are elevations showing the pre-fire configuration and as restored. On the right-hand side are two sections of the pre-fire façade and a section as restored.

37 *Sketch of the decoration of a door, probably in the Saloon*

Priv. Corr. XIII.C.3.107
Pencil and pen

Dated: *Wotton House, Sunday 2d Dec 1821*

This sketch, in Soane's hand, relates to the door of one of the three large rooms at the ground floor (the coved ceiling indicates that it could be the Saloon). The sketch design for the door shows two columns flanking the door and supporting a pediment. Below this, he has sketched in a more 'Grecian' pediment with acroteria, and an unfinished plan showing how the column is separated from the wall.

38 *Rough sketches in Soane's hand of the elevation of the Entrance Hall*

Priv. Corr. XIII.C.3.108
Pen

In the top part of this sheet are two complete elevations which relate to the first proposal for the Hall (Cats 8 & 9), presented to Buckingham by Soane at Stowe on 17 and 18 November 1820.

The two sketches present different proposals. The left-hand one shows three storeys, whereas in the right-hand one, the middle level is reduced to a decorative feature. Between these two sketches is an unfinished sketch of the elevation of the Hall.

The upper proposal for the central arch consists of two niches separated by a column on a pedestal. The left-hand solution on the lower part of the sheet presents two columns flanking a niche, above a wide pedestal. The last alternative is closer to the later proposals, with paired columns on a basement surmounted by a trophy.

39 *Account of the masons' work at Wotton*

Priv. Corr. XIII.C.3.110 verso
Pen

This shows the back of the account on which Soane has sketched the chamber floor and lantern of the tribune.

40 *Letter from Thomas Wyatt to James Cook*

Cpbd F/ii/12

Dated: *Oxford, March 21st 1822*

The mason Thomas Wyatt, who worked with his father Richard Wyatt at Wotton House, writes to the Clerk of Works, James Cook. The letter is about work matters, i.e. an estimate for paving and a complaint about the quality of the stone. The final sentence is a charming reminder that there were more important things in life than work: 'I have sent you a few sausages & regret that I could not procure more of them being all they had this morning'.

41–44 *Exercise books used by plasterers at Wotton*

Cpbd F/ii/4; Cpbd F/ii/7; Cpbd F/ii/8; Cpbd F/ii/9

These four books record the work done by the plasterers at Wotton House but they are most interesting for their ornate covers with prints and poems. One is embellished with 'Morning, or the Rising of the Sun', and another with 'The Negro's complaint'.

45 *The 3rd Duke of Buckingham and Chandos returning to Wotton House from India in February 1881*

Black & white photographic print (248 x 304)
Collection of Mr and Mrs Gladstone

The 3rd Duke spent five years in India as Governor-General of Madras. A lavish reception party was organised for his visit to his ancestral seat and the moment of his 'Happy return to Wotton' is captured in this remarkable photograph. Above the doorway hangs the Buckingham coat of arms (see Cat.47). The event was covered at length in an article in the *Buckinghamshire Herald*. The Duke concluded his address at the celebratory luncheon by thanking his tenants and neighbours for their 'kind welcome, doubly welcome to me now I have returned to a place where I have spent so many years, and so many happy years'.

This photograph shows the chimneystacks as built by Soane. The present chimneys are lower, having been altered during the restoration work of the 1950s and 60s.

45

46 John Buckler (1770–1851)

View of the entrance front of Wotton House, 1818

Watercolour (445 x 597)
Collection of Mr and Mrs David Gladstone

Pre-fire Wotton is captured in this fine topographical view by John Buckler. The high attic storey (later lowered by Soane) and the nine prominent chimneystacks are clearly visible. There is a similar version of this watercolour in Vol.8 of Lysons' *History of Buckinghamshire* (Cat.50). (see p.9)

47 & 48 *Coats of arms*

Oil on canvas (both 720 x 860)
Buckinghamshire County Museum
Lit: Anon., *A Description of the Shields of Arms recently put up in the Hall of Wotton House in the County of Bucks*. London, 1823

The hanging canopy in Soane's new tribune at Wotton was designed to take eighteen shields together with these two large coats of arms. Cat.47, the Duke of Buckingham's arms, was originally placed opposite the entrance. Cat.48 is the coat of arms for the Marquis of Chandos and this was placed in a panel over the Front door. They were removed to the County Record Office in the early 20th century, prior to the remodelling work by A S G Butler.

47

Reproduced courtesy of Buckinghamshire County Museum

49 Ptolemy Dean

Reconstruction of Soane's tribune

Pen and watercolour (420 x 295)
Collection of the artist
Lit: *Country Life*, May 2004, p. 112

Soane's tribune at Wotton was lost when the house was remodelled in 1929–30. No photographs or artists' views of the space survive and there are frustratingly few drawings of the final design in Soane's collection.

This perspective view of the vanished space, commissioned by *Country Life*, has been carefully reconstructed using information from the original drawings. The later fireplace and the later 2nd floor staircase flight have been included but the other elements (and scale) are based entirely on Soane's designs.

50 Daniel Lysons (1762–1834) and Samuel Lysons (1763–1819)

Magna Britannia; Being a Concise Topographical Account of the Several Counties of Great Britain, Vol.I, Part III, History of Buckinghamshire, Vol.8. London 1813 & 1836. Illustrations by John Buckler, Thomas Sandby and others

Printed book with watercolour illustrations
(677 x 467)
The late Sir Paul Getty KBE, the Wormsley Library

This lavish extra-illustrated volume was part of a set of eight covering the county of Buckinghamshire. The volumes were prepared at 'unlimited expense' for William Wyndham Grenville of Dropmore (1759–1834) from the existing Lysons volumes published in 1813. Grenville died two years before the completion of the series but left instructions for the set to be given to his nephew the 1st Duke of Buckingham and Chandos in memory of his father. This volume, the last of the series, features Wotton House and its landscape. The topographical watercolour views are by John Buckler (see also Cat.46).

51 Sir James Thornhill (1675–1734)

Wotton House. View from the south-east, c. 1715

Pen and wash (210 x 300)
Buckinghamshire County Museum
Lit: John Harris, *The Artist and the Country House*, London and New York, 1985, p.259

In the early 1710s Thornhill spent three years at Wotton painting the staircase and Saloon. This drawing, with its innovative diagonal perspective, was made during this period. In *The Artist and the Country House* John Harris speculates that Thornhill might even have been the architect of the house.

51

Reproduced courtesy of Buckinghamshire County Museum

The upper level of the Hall in 1949 © *Country Life* Picture Library